All My Liberty
Theology of the Spiritual Exercises

by JOHN A. HARDON, S.J.
Professor of Dogmatic Theology
West Baden College, West Baden Springs, Indiana

All

My Liberty

Theology of the Spiritual Exercises

THE NEWMAN PRESS • WESTMINSTER, MARYLAND
1959

Imprimi Potest: WILLIAM J. SCHMIDT, S.J.
Provincial of the Chicago Province, S.J.
September 23, 1958

Nihil Obstat: FRANCIS J. CONNELL, C.SS.R., S.T.D.
Censor Deputatus

Imprimatur: GEORGE L. LEECH, D.D.
Bishop of Harrisburg
June 12, 1959

Acknowledgments

THE AUTHOR wishes most of all to thank two persons whose generous cooperation in the writing of this volume covers a period of more than twenty years. As novice master, Rev. William J. Young, S.J., gave the writer a love for the Spiritual Exercises and a veneration for their Author without which the present study would never have been made. As master of tertians, Rev. Aloysius C. Kemper, S.J., developed these sentiments and strengthened their ascetical and dogmatic foundations. Moreover both men have read the manuscript with painstaking care and offered valuable recommendations, drawn from their rich experience in Ignatian spirituality.

To Brother Eugene J. Nevins, S.J., is due a special note of gratitude for typing and setting up the manuscript. His patient and expert assistance was indispensable.

Contents

Part One
KEY MEDITATIONS OF THE EXERCISES

Part Two
IGNATIAN IDEALS AND METHODOLOGY

Relics and Images, Saints and Indulgences 154
Fasting, Abstinence, and Exterior Penances 157
Obedience of the Intellect 159
Respect for Obedience under Trial 163
Positive and Scholastic Theology 165
Prudence in Evaluating Sanctity 167
Perfect Submission to the Church's Magisterium 169
Some Cautions on Predestination 171
Faith and Good Works 173
Grace and Free Will 175
The Fear and Love of God 177

APPENDIX I: SELECTIONS FROM THE TEXT OF THE EXERCISES 181

First Principle and Foundation 181
Sin: Angelic, Original, and Personal 181
The Kingdom of Christ 186
Two Standards 187
Three Classes of Men 189
Three Kinds of Humility 190
Two Ways of Making an Election 191
Directions for Amendment and Reformation in One's State of Life 193
Contemplation to Attain the Love of God 194

APPENDIX II: APOSTOLIC CONSTITUTION OF PIUS XI DECLARING ST. IGNATIUS PATRON OF ALL SPIRITUAL EXERCISES 197

INDEX 201

Introduction

THREE kinds of books have been written on the Spiritual Exercises, each with a different purpose and reading public in mind. Most numerous are the commentaries for retreat masters that offer a series of meditations in outline to be given to others. Another type is the familiar manual which develops all the reflections and practically supplies for the retreat master. Combinations of both types have also been published. Finally there are studies on the Exercises themselves, their history, theology or psychology, which aim beyond the immediate function of making or giving a retreat to discover ascetical values that are hidden beneath the surface.

The present volume belongs to the third class, as a modern theological appraisal of the Spiritual Exercises intended to facilitate their use in giving retreats, and to give retreatants, whether priests, religious or the laity, a deeper insight into the treasures of the Exercises in order to make them more profitable. Also, retreats already made will take on a new and more incisive meaning. The need for such a volume appears from the practical absence, at least in English, of a professional study of the master-ideas around which the Exercises are built and in which their special value for sanctification reputedly consists.

Before entering into the analysis, however, it will be useful to examine a few preliminary facts and ideas. The Spiritual Exercises have a long and celebrated history that may be traced to apostolic times. Yet their existence in the present form and the universal acceptance of a closed retreat as an institution in the Catholic Church are due to St. Ignatius. Another book could be written on the historical antecedents and subsequent influence of the Ignatian Exercises. But even a short review of the background may explain why a closer study of their contents should be made. Any instrument or practice which the highest authority in the Church placed "in the front rank of all the means that help towards Christian perfection" deserves our careful investigation.

ORIGINS AND SCOPE OF THE SPIRITUAL EXERCISES

In a popular and general sense, the term "Spiritual Exercises" refers to all the practices of piety that are commonly used to foster personal sanctity. But more specifically it means a period of time, of varying length, during which a person devotes himself exclusively to prayer and meditation and, as far as possible, in seclusion from other duties and cares.

The example of Christ in the desert and the Apostles in the cenacle waiting for the Holy Spirit inspired the custom among the early Christians of selected groups retiring into the wilderness for prayer and fasting during the season of Lent. Outstanding among the early promoters of these lenten retreats was St. Euthymius (377–473), whose feast is celebrated on January 20. Historians of the patristic age believe that the practice was quite universal from the sixth to the eighth centuries. In the Middle Ages most of the monasteries had special rooms set aside for retreatants, who were lay people from the world or hermits dedicated to a life of solitude, until the general decline of monasticism also affected these "spiritual vacations" and suspended a movement that was in operation for more than a thousand years.

As a reaction to the religious upheaval of the fourteenth century (the age of Wyclif and Hus), high-minded persons like Gerard Groote (1340–1384) betook themselves for a week or more to some monastery and there inaugurated what has since become known as the *Devotio Moderna*, which identified spiritual perfection with the imitation of Jesus Christ. St. Ignatius Loyola inherited the spirit of this *Devotio*, which he personalized by his own reflections and mystical experience and reduced to a set of definite meditations and organized into a logical synthesis which he called the Spiritual Exercises. Another feature he added was to prescribe that this ascetical experience be made under the guidance of a competent spiritual director.

"There is no other work of Catholic literature," says the Protestant Fülöp-Miller, "which, for its historical effect, can be compared with Ignatius' little book of the Exercises." Yet its strategy is very simple. In the first stage, called the First Week, after studying the Principle and Foundation as the norm by which all human actions must be judged, the exercitant is faced with the spectacle of sin and inspired with a horror for anything which could hinder his journey to God. Following on this spiritual purgation, Ignatius presents Jesus Christ as the perfect model of God's service, in the act of calling others to follow Him; at the same time he disposes the retreatant to set his affections and all other things in order after the example of his Master. In the Third Week, the author of the Exercises seeks to deepen the union of the soul with her Lord by penetrating her with the sentiments which He felt in the Passion and thus preparing her, in the last Week, for the "Contemplation to obtain Divine Love." The experience has been compared to reliving the life of Christ in miniature by passing through the same sequence of suffering, crucifixion and death which He endured, and finally entering with Him into everlasting joy.

St. Ignatius wrote the Exercises with this purpose in mind and organized its contents accordingly. Consequently it is not a book to be read, and less still a systematic exposition of ascetical principles. The structure of the book was outlined at Manresa (1522), where his mind was so enlightened on the truths of revelation that, in his own words, "he seemed to be possessed of a new intellect, with such conviction that, from what he had seen, it would be his duty to lay down his life for the mysteries of faith even if the Scriptures did not bear witness to them." Further experiences and more study served to develop the outline. Ignatius also expanded the original form by reshaping the points of meditation and adding directives to help others use the book as a retreat manual. In this stage of revision we can trace the influence of the *Imitation of Christ*, of the *Life of Christ* by Ludolph of Saxony, of the *Golden Legend* by Jacopo de Voragine and certain manuals of devotion like the *Ejercitatorio* of the Spanish Benedictine, Cisneros. But in all these the influence is seen to be psychological rather than literal, with the possible exception of the *Imitation* which Ignatius is known to have treasured next to the Bible.

PAPAL APPROVAL AND DIFFUSION

By a strange coincidence, the Exercises were first solemnly approved by Pope Paul III on July 31, 1548, just eight years, to the day, before the death of St. Ignatius. The papal brief *Pastoralis Officii* thus began a series of more than six hundred testimonials by thirty-five sovereign pontiffs, notably the late Pius XI, whose devotion to the Exercises dated from his earliest days in the priesthood. He had seen their effectiveness during his thirty years' association with a lay retreat house, and later on, as Pope, declared that he was led by the Exercises "to adopt a more perfect way of life." In answer to the request of more than six hundred bishops, in 1922 he appointed St. Ignatius "the heavenly patron of all Spiritual Exercises," and identified him as "the first to begin to teach a certain system and special method of going through spiritual retreats." Since the terms of the apostolic constitution are similar to those which Leo XIII had used in declaring St. Thomas patron of Catholic schools, some commentators conclude that St. Ignatius enjoys a preeminence in the science of spirituality comparable to that of "the universal and common doctor" in the field of theological science.

Although the original Spanish text of the Exercises is lost, we still have an authentic copy, annotated by Ignatius, which goes by the name of "autograph." Present estimates show that the Exercises have been translated into twenty-two languages, running into more than three hundred editions. There is a current listing of over eight hundred authors who have written one or more volumes of commentary, so that the average output is calculated at one edition of text or commentary every month for the last four hundred years.

Originally the Exercises were given to private individuals. Jesuit colleges in the sixteenth century had special rooms reserved for visiting retreatants. But almost from the beginning separate retreat houses were also in operation, of which the first on record was in Siena, opened on a temporary basis in 1538. The first permanent institution was opened at Alcalá in 1553, followed soon after at Cologne (1561), Louvain (1569), and Val de Rosal (1570). A famous retreat house for deaf mutes was built at Milan in 1579 by St. Charles Borromeo, who made Ignatian asceticism the spearhead of the Counter-Reformation which he promoted during the reign of his uncle, Pope Pius IV. Already in the sixteenth century, the Exercises were used in all the countries of Europe, and introduced to America and the Far East. Among the retreatants were priests and religious in every grade of the hierarchy, including members of the oldest orders in the Church, and the laity from all classes of society.

Group retreats, which began in the 1500's among priests and religious, were developed still further in the next century by men like Vincent de Paul and Francis de Sales, who extended the concept of Christian perfection beyond the cloister and through the Exercises placed it within the reach of all the faithful. St. Vincent de Paul is known to have given the Exercises personally to more than 20,000 people.

An important contributing factor to the popularity of retreats in the eighteenth century was the high commendation they received from successive Roman Pontiffs. Benedict XIV, for example, prescribed the Exercises for young men entering a seminary, for all clerics before their ordination, for monks and hermits during canonical visitation, for missionaries in England and the Orient; and in a long papal document, he observed that "since the time when St. Ignatius composed the marvelous Book of the Exercises, there is scarcely a religious order in the Church that has not adopted this salutary practice," for its own members and as a "fruitful instrument" in the apostolate.

The suppression of the Society of Jesus did incalculable harm to the retreat movement and might have injured the cause irreparably except for the zealous promotion by men and women who had previously made the Exercises and recognized their high potentialities. Thus St. Alphonsus Liguori and the Redemptorists in Italy, Bishop Johann Sailer in Germany, and Mary Antonia de la Paz in South America kept the movement alive and ready for its unprecedented expansion in the last century. Religious congregations were even started for the sole purpose of directing or assisting with retreats for the laity, like the Society of Our Lady of the Cenacle, founded at La Louvesc in 1826. It was at the Cenacle in Milan that the convent chaplain, Achille Ratti, came to appreciate the extraordinary value of the Exercises and later on, as Pius XI, promoted them to the limit of his papal authority.

Three names that stand out for their contribution to the theory and practice of the Spiritual Exercise are Roothaan, Ravignan and Watrigant. As twenty-first general of the Society of Jesus, John Roothaan published a Latin translation and commentary that have become standard sources; moreover, his insistence on the true Ignatian spirit in giving retreats merited him the title of "restorer of the Spiritual Exercises," following the obscuration of this spirit during the suppression of the Society. Père de Ravignan, who succeeded Lacordaire as preacher at Notre Dame, used the Exercises to transform the spiritual life of the French élite, and thus proved their effectiveness even among the sophisticated classes of society. The Belgian Watrigant spent a lifetime assembling the world's largest library on the Exercises, over 8000 volumes, and in 1906 founded the periodical *Bibliothèque des Exercices* devoted to a study and popularization of the accumulated riches of four centuries since Manresa.

The modern development is without parallel in the history of the Church for the number and variety of persons who make annual retreats that are somehow inspired by the Ignatian Exercises. According to Canon Law, priests are obliged to "make the spiritual exercises at least every three years," religious men and women once every year, and those preparing to receive Tonsure and Major Orders, for three to six days. Among the laity, the scope of the retreat movement is beyond calculation. The Society of Jesus alone gives the Exercises in closed retreats to more than one million persons annually.

Comparable to the world picture, the Exercises have an American history that goes back to the earliest missionaries in the New World. What appears to have been the first lay retreat in North America was made in 1640 by a crippled Indian convert in French Canada whose retreat election, according to the *Jesuit Relations*, was to give up the practice of smoking. In three centuries, the use of the Spiritual Exercises has grown into a national movement that for large-scale efficiency and organization is probably unequalled in the Catholic Church. Four hundred institutions in forty-six States, operating on a permanent or seasonal basis, give retreats of three to eight days to an average of more than half a million men and women every year. During his visit to the United States, Cardinal Pacelli was so impressed that after his elevation to the papacy he told the American bishops how pleased he was to see "the Spiritual Exercises of St. Ignatius followed with great devotion in your closed retreats," which he assumed are mostly according to the Ignatian method.

PRIMARY SOURCES OF INTERPRETATION AND DOCTRINE

Since the turn of the century, the basis for any scientific study of the Exercises is the prodigious *Monumenta Ignatiana*, published at Madrid in twenty-two volumes and containing all but a fraction of the extant writings of St. Ignatius and about him by his contemporaries. The critical text of the Exercises, in four parallel columns, gives a synoptic view of the variants, generally minor, between the Spanish autograph and three Latin versions. St. Ignatius also left three sets of instructions, called Directories, on how to conduct the Exercises; one set personally composed by him and the other two under his orders or dictation.

The editors of the *Monumenta* give the complete text of twelve additional Directories, written after the death of St. Ignatius and before the end of the sixteenth century. Of these the most valuable was made by John Polanco, the contemporary and confidant of St. Ignatius; the most widely known and currently used was published in 1599. Taken together these Directories established a tradition that is certainly unique in the history of ascetical writing. They insure to the modern student of the Exercises an authentic interpretation of their author's mind and spirituality.

Another sixteenth century document of great interpretative value is the lengthy *Apologia* of Nadal, friend of Ignatius, who defended the Exercises against professional critics and in so doing elaborated on their whole theological structure. His defense of the Ignatian concept of indifference, spiritual consolation and predestination remains unsurpassed to this day:

When at Manresa he wrote a good part of the Exercises, Ignatius had not yet done any studying. Later he devoted himself to study with an incredible zeal, first in Spain and then at the University of Paris, which was then so celebrated throughout the Christian world. For several years he followed the course in arts and the course in theology with the greatest application, rare constancy and success. His studies finished, he gathered these early pages [of the

Exercises], added a good many things and systematically arranged the whole.

From this Nadal argued to the supernatural assistance Ignatius received in the cave of Manresa and the years of studious reflection he gave to improving his spiritual classic.

Early in the seventeenth century, Francis Suarez again defended the Exercises for theological orthodoxy and, like Nadal, developed their implications in his treatise *De Religione*. "There is nothing doctrinal in the Exercises," he wrote, "which can be called into question. Their content is either a restatement of certain and dogmatic principles, or derived from the more common teaching of theologians."

Apart from the inspired books of the New Testament, the two principal sources of doctrine in the Spiritual Exercises were Saints Augustine and Thomas Aquinas. Ignatius' reverence for the African bishop may be seen from the frequent quotations in his letters and the practical certainty that the Rule of St. Augustine was among the monastic models on which he built his own religious institute. In a sense, the whole tenor of Ignatian asceticism, with its accent on the conflict of good and evil and personal devotion to Christ, reflects Augustinian theology.

However the proximate source of doctrinal orientation in the Exercises was Thomas Aquinas. From his first contact with the *Summa* while studying with the Dominicans at Paris, Ignatius turned as by instinct to the Angelic Doctor. When writing the Constitutions of his order, he prescribed for the teaching of theology "the scholastic doctrine of St. Thomas." This injunction anticipated by three centuries the present law of the Church on clerical and theological studies. It also simplifies the doctrinal analysis of the Exercises by revealing them as an ascetical counterpart of the *Summa Theologica*.

SPIRITUAL EFFICACY

Among the hundreds of papal commendations, the most significant is the encyclical *Mens Nostra* of Pope Pius XI, is-

sued in 1929 as a memorial to the Church on his golden jubi-
lee in the priesthood. He gave several reasons why "of all the
methods for making the Spiritual Exercises the one introduced
by St. Ignatius has ever held the foremost place." For our purpose these reasons may serve as an apologia for the present
volume.

Without implying the slightest reflection on other retreat
methods "which laudably adhere to the principles of sound
Catholic asceticism," the Pope singled out as the first quality
of the Ignatian Exercises "the excellence of their doctrine,
which is altogether free from the perils and errors of false
mysticism." We shall later expand on this feature of ascetical
security. Here it is enough to mention that wherever mystical
doctrine departed from the path of orthodoxy it was in one
of two directions, either so stressing the operations of grace
as to fall into quietism which makes the human will completely passive in the hands of God, or at least so concentrating
on direct inspiration as to obviate the need for external guidance from legitimate ecclesiastical authority. The Ignatian Exercises from beginning to end forestall both tendencies by
their whole approach to the spiritual life. Their insistence on
the autonomous power of human liberty and our capacity for
high generosity precludes the danger of ascetical passivism
which, for St. Ignatius, was almost a contradiction in terms.
And their devotion to the Church as the Spouse of Christ and
infallible teacher of mankind, concretized in the Rules of Orthodoxy, will not be lost on the most casual retreatant. In fact,
Ignatius' requirement of a competent retreat master with elaborate directives on how to lead a person through the Exercises
became essential for making a true retreat.

The second quality which commends the Exercises is their
"admirable facility of being adaptable to any status or condition of men, whether devoted to contemplation in the cloister
or leading an active life in the affairs of the world." Historical
evidence supports this judgment, that every rank and level of
society, in the priesthood, cloister and the laity, has followed

the Exercises with great benefit to personal sanctity and apostolic work. Behind the adaptability was the rare insight that Ignatius had into the basic conflicts and aspirations of our nature, which he derived by going through almost every stage of human experience, from a dissipated youth during which he was once brought to trial for "grave and enormous crimes," to later conversion and spiritual maturity that culminated in the highest form of mysticism. Another reason was the care that Ignatius took over a period of twenty years to implement the meditations with copious directives, rules and practical suggestions for the retreat master. In other words, by the express intention of their author, the Exercises are not a rigid code but a flexible mode of spirituality. "They should be adapted," he tells the director, "to the disposition of those who wish to make them, depending on their age, education or capacity. In like manner, according to each one's desires and dispositions, he should be given what is most helpful and profitable to him." Thus if a retreatant has "not much strength of character," only the early meditations on sin and hell are recommended. Or, if the director sees a person making the Exercises with great fervor, he must warn him against any rash promises that might later have to be rescinded.

There is also an "apt coordination of the various parts in the Exercises," and a "marvelously clear order in the meditation of truths that follow naturally one from another." The consequent appeal to the mind is spontaneous, and serves the double purpose of concentrating attention on a single object and integrating disparate elements in the spiritual life around the focal idea of loving God in the person of Jesus Christ. According to reliable testimony the Communists have adopted the structure and sequence of the Exercises, substituted Lenin for Christ, and are giving a Marxist "retreat" of forty days in silence on the principle and foundation of dialectical materialism. In making the Exercises, says the Protestant writer Evelyn Underhill, "we feel the drive and determination of the soldier, whose natural attitude is the attitude of attack, and who shirks nothing and forgets nothing which can contribute to the chosen end. It is a spiritual drill, directed to a definite result; but a drill which implies and rests on a profound and vivid understanding of the business of the soul."

But the highest quality of the Exercises is not their freedom from pseudo-mysticism, nor their logic and adaptability. Their greatest value lies in the power they have "to lead a man through the safe paths of abnegation and the removal of bad habits to the very summit of prayer and divine love." This is proved experimentally by the changes in moral conduct and spiritual conviction that a single retreat has effected in the lives of thousands of persons. Among the saints, Charles Borromeo was led by the Exercises "to adopt a more perfect form of life," Francis de Sales "to serve God with the greatest possible fidelity," and Teresa of Avila to become "the mistress of lofty contemplation." On the level of ordinary piety the experience of every retreat master shows the disproportion, sometimes nearly miraculous, between the time and human effort spent in making the Exercises and the marvelous results they produce. Contributing to this efficacy are many factors that the following pages hope to elucidate. But one thing hard to analyze and yet certainly operative is a mysterious element which Pius XI called "a divine instinct." It explains the composition of what some have described as "a book of human destiny," which drew on resources beyond the natural capacity of its author; it may also explain its influence in terms of a supernatural force that God reserves for the chosen instruments of His grace.

I

Key Meditations of the Exercises

1

Principle and Foundation of the Spiritual Life

THE Principle and Foundation is not only chronologically the first prayerful consideration of the Spiritual Exercises and logically the basis of all the meditations which follow. It synthesizes St. Ignatius' doctrine of Christian perfection. There is an emphasis on man's free cooperation with divine grace, a logical adaptation of the best means to a desired end, and a concept of generosity in dealing with God which many theologians consider the essential elements of Ignatian spirituality.

Three writers with whom St. Ignatius was familiar are commonly mentioned as possible sources from which he derived the wording if not the doctrine of the Principle and Foundation.

Erasmus of Rotterdam in his *Enchiridion Militis Christiani* speaks of choosing the best means of attaining salvation, "If you are running straight to the goal, whatever you meet on the way should be used if it helps and rejected if it hinders your course to the *summum bonum*." But Ignatius disliked Erasmus after only a short reading and in later life would not even handle the man's writings because they "froze the spirit of his soul."[1]

Ludolph of Saxony is a more likely source because of St. Ignatius' devotion to the Carthusian's *Vita Christi*, in which

[1] *Monumenta Historica*, "Monumenta Ignatiana: Exercitia Spiritualia," Madrid, 1919, p. 131.

3

the honor due to creatures was compared with the glory that we owe the Creator.

However the most favored influence is Thomas a Kempis' *Imitation of Christ*, whose impact on the Spiritual Exercises was deep and unmistakable. The core ideas of indifference and a pure intention are certainly derived from a Kempis, where Ignatius read: "Son, I must be your supreme and ultimate end, if you desire to be truly happy. By this intention shall your affections be purified, which too often are irregularly bent upon yourself and things created."[2]

THEMATIC ANALYSIS

Although the two words, Principle and Foundation, are almost synonymous, there is a shade of difference between them. The opening exercise may be considered theoretically or practically. In the first sense it may be called "the Principle from which everything else in the Exercises is more elaborately deduced, which intimately affects all the subsequent matter and to which the whole of the Exercises may be reduced." Taken practically, it is the Foundation "on which the whole weight of the Spiritual Exercises, the whole structure of the spiritual life is built. This doctrine on the end of man is the basic truth on which depend the other truths to be proposed and from which they inevitably and securely arise as its fruit."[3]

We can distinguish four elementary truths in the Principle and Foundation which form the master plan of the Exercises:

End of man for which he was created.

Means to attain this end.

Difficulty in the choice of these means.

Indifference of will in order to expedite the choice.

[2] *Imitation of Christ*, Book III, Chapter 9.

[3] *Opera Spiritualia Joannis P. Roothaan*, Vol. II, Romae, 1936, p. 32. In the same context, Roothaan stresses the importance of the prayer of petition from the very beginning of the Spiritual Exercises, "earnestly begging God for light to clearly understand the primary truth expressed in the Foundation, and grace for the will spontaneously to accept the practical conclusions derived from its serious consideration. Above all the exercitant should apply this truth and its essential consequences to *himself.*" *Ibid.*, p. 35.

The connection between these elements is perfectly logical. Given the fact that man was created to save his soul by praising, honoring and serving God and that all other things were made to help him attain this end, the first conclusion is that creatures should be used according as they help in the prosecution of man's purpose in life. Implicit at this point is the reality that man as a free agent must choose among various creatures, and that on this choice depends his eternal salvation. It is further implied that the choice will not be easy to make and therefore a second conclusion follows: in order to facilitate the right choice we must cultivate a spirit of indifference or detachment, and not allow mere natural tendencies to determine the selection of creatures.

The same theme reappears at strategic points in the Exercises. During the First Week the history of man shows a reversal of the Principle and Foundation, a departure from God in sin and its terrible consequences in death and hell. In the Second Week there is a Christological concretization of the Foundation in the contrast between Christ and Satan and its psychological synthesis in the Three Classes, the Three Degrees and the Election. In the Third Week the Passion of Christ to confirm the Election, following the example of Christ who chose the opposite of that to which we are naturally inclined. The Fourth Week is additional motivation, closing with the Contemplation for Obtaining Love, where the service of God (from the Foundation) proves to be really love, and "the other things on the face of the earth" are shown to exist only to help us grow in the love of God.

THEOLOGICAL ISSUES

Since the main issues of the Principle and Foundation are the common possession of the whole Exercises, they will not be treated exhaustively here but are taken up again in the analysis of subsequent meditations. Also to be noted is the approach to questions involving an interpretation of St. Ignatius' mind on a particular point, which can be discovered only

by an appeal to historical sources. Once this has been established, we may analyze the meaning of certain concepts like
indifference, detachment and the purpose of creatures according to standard ascetical norms.

The Principle and Foundation is Supernatural: From both
internal and external evidence it is clear that the truths enun-
ciated in the Principle and Foundation are supernatural, being
derived from revelation and referring to an order of reality
above nature. Nowhere in the Exercises does St. Ignatius suggest a transition from considering man only philosophically in
the Foundation and then theologically, according to faith, in
the subsequent meditations. Moreover by recognizing that
man has a "bias" in the direction of things naturally pleasing
but not necessarily conducive to his last end, St. Ignatius implies the existence of a fallen human nature, which is clearly
a supernatural concept. Accordingly, the salvation of one's
soul, in the Foundation, means the Beatific Vision; the praise
and service of God involve the whole body of Christian faith
and morals; the "other things on the face of the earth" which
are to assist man include supernatural realities like the Church
and the sacraments; and the acquisition of indifference requires
the help of divine grace.

Two Aspects of Man's Relation to God: There are two ways
in which the creation of man may be considered, depending on
what aspect is emphasized. The stress may be placed on the
truth that "Man was created," or on the fact that he is "to
save his soul." In the first case, God is viewed in relation to
man as the efficient cause of his existence, in the second as
final cause. Both are equally true and both should be treated
in the Exercises, but they represent different viewpoints and
in practice will have to be balanced and adapted to the retreatants' needs. The difference can be expressed schematically:

	GOD AS EFFICIENT CAUSE	GOD AS FINAL CAUSE
Meaning	God made man out of nothing by an act of His sovereign will.	God made man for union with Himself in the Beatific Vision.

Divine attribute emphasized	God's power and wisdom.	God's infinite love.
Consequences for man	Complete submission to God as Creator and Lord.	Gratitude to God for His infinite generosity.
Response on the part of man	Fidelity to the laws of God in perfect obedience.	Desire to grow in union with God and to share this union with others.
Motive stressed	Reverential fear of God's justice, for infringement of His rights.	Love of God's goodness, to be possessed for all eternity.

Attention should be drawn to the value of taking cognizance of the final cause of creation. Man's origin can be known by reason alone, and by itself says nothing about his elevation to the supernatural order or the real destiny to which he is called; whereas a proper understanding of his destiny in the Beatific Vision gives added, profound intelligibility to the praise and service of God which are the necessary means to its attainment. A certain emphasis on beatitude as the end of man also puts the right corrective to any suspicion of advantage to God from our obedience to His will; once it becomes evident that God did not create man to profit from his service but to benefit the man who serves Him. In the words of the Vatican Council, "The one and only true God created both orders of creatures in the same way out of nothing, the spiritual or angelic world and the corporeal or visible universe, and afterwards He formed the creature man, who in a way belongs to both orders, as he is composed of spirit and body—in order to manifest His perfection through the benefits which He bestows on creatures, not to intensify His happiness nor to acquire any perfection."[4] Creation is the ultimate of divine altruism.

The Meaning of Indifference: Ignatian indifference is a quality of the will, and specifically the perfection of freedom from internal determination caused by an inordinate love or fear of created things. The immediate source of this inordination is

---

[4] Denzinger *Enchiridion*, 1783. (Subsequent references to this collection of ecclesiastical documents will be identified only by their editor, Denzinger, and the corresponding number of the document.)

concupiscence, both carnal and spiritual. In carnal concupiscence where the sense appetite does not fully submit to the rational will, the latter inclines to embrace whatever pleases and shun whatever gives pain to the senses independently of the dictates of right reason. In spiritual concupiscence the disorder is the same, except that here the will tends to seek whatever pleases and avoid whatever pains the spiritual faculties, the mind and will, independently of right reason and the teachings of faith. However the ultimate explanation of this conflict between subjective desire and objective good lies deeper than original sin which deprived man of the gift of integrity, with immunity from concupiscence; it is mysteriously bound up with man's condition in the state of probation, where he has the power of choice between moral good and evil.

There are two kinds of constraint which militate against volitional freedom and, on occasion, may suppress it completely: the external coercion of physical force, of which there is no question in the Foundation, and the internal compulsion of natural tendencies which desire autonomous expression without subordination to higher values. St. Ignatius recognizes the power of these internal desires and therefore urges their habitual control as the *sine qua non* of Christian perfection. In proportion as a man frees himself from their tyranny, he enjoys indifference or liberty to follow that which his mind, enlightened by revelation, tells him is most conducive to the end for which he was created. Consequently, "to make ourselves indifferent" means the cultivation of both intellect and will: of the intellect to have it see with conviction the destiny to which man has been called and the necessary means to be taken to arrive there; and of the will to deliver it from domination by its impulses. For although indifference belongs primarily to the will, it also includes the perfection of the mind which clearly perceives what is objectively good or evil on the road to salvation and so presents its vision to the emancipated will for acceptance or rejection.

Indifference a Matter of Precept or Counsel? A disputed

question arises on the necessity of this indifference, whether it is obligatory under pain of sin, or only a counsel offered for acceptance by more generous souls. Those who favor the first opinion say that, "Universal indifference is a disposition necessary to perform duties indispensable for salvation," and "to fail in indifference with regard to a single creature is to withdraw from our last end."⁵ Warrant for this attitude is found in the standard text of the Foundation, which says that "it is necessary that we should make ourselves indifferent."⁶ Another group believes that Ignatian indifference is "neither a necessity of salvation nor a necessity of duty," that "it is a question of fulfilling a condition, not absolutely for attaining our end . . . but for the observance of the rule of wisdom and of perfection in the use of creatures."⁷ The argument is based on Nadal's *Apology* for the Exercises, where this confidant of Ignatius states that "we should never have thought it a sin to fail in indifference; we say only that it is preferable to make oneself indifferent in order to achieve the purpose of the Exercises. . . . If, therefore, we say that indifference is necessary, we are only giving a counsel, we are not imposing an obligation."⁸ Unless understood as a counsel, what room is there for the heroism demanded by the Spiritual Exercises, and how explain the Third Class of Men or the Third Mode of Humility if indifference obliges everyone under pain of sin?

The two positions can be reconciled, provided we take neither one exclusively. In favor of the first opinion it must be granted that a certain degree of indifference towards creatures is necessary to keep the moral law and the basic precepts of the Gospel; unless controlled, our natural tendencies will betray us into sin. It would be a mistake, however, to suppose that this is the only kind of indifference taught by the Prin-

⁵ Victor Mercier, *Manuel des Exercices*, Poitiers, 1894, p. 205. Also Janvier Bucceroni, *Exercices Spirituels*, 1904, p. 64.

⁶ Mercier, *op. cit.*, p. 33.

⁷ Pierre Bouvier, *The Authentic Interpretation of the Foundation*, Bourges (MS edition), 1922, pp. 24–25.

⁸ *Monumenta Historica*, "Chronicon Polanci," III, Madrid, 1895.

ciple and Foundation. In support of the second opinion it is equally true that the specific indifference ambitioned by the Exercises extends to creatures which may be chosen or rejected without sin. Here the mistake would be to overlook or underestimate that prior indifference which safeguards obedience to the commandments of God, since the spiritual perfection of the counsels presupposes that the substance of sanctity in the precepts has been firmly secured.

Creatures as External Graces of God: A legitimate interpretation of the function of creatures in the plan of God considers them so many graces given to man as the instruments of salvation. If we ask what purpose the Creator had in making "all other things on the face of the earth," we are told, "to aid man in the prosecution of the end for which he was created." If we further ask the meaning of grace, we call it a supernatural (undeserved) gift received by a rational creature from God in order to attain the Beatific Vision. In other words, the two coincide, so that we may look upon the activity of God as embracing all time and all things, operating without ceasing and with divine surety for the salvation of souls. Every creature, no matter how trifling or apparently fortuitous, is really, in its way, a predestined means to lead men to their supernatural end. They are all graces, technically called external, to distinguish them from internal graces which are immediately and specially received from God in the intellect and will.

In answer to the question, then: What is an external grace?, we say it is every creature that is not an internal grace of God, as explained by St. Thomas in his commentary on the words of St. Paul, "We know that for those who love God all things work together unto good, for those who, according to His purpose, are saints through His call" (Rom. 8:28). According to St. Thomas, "The Apostle is here showing how the Holy Spirit assists us through external events, directing them to our good. . . . Evidence of this is the fact that whatever there is in the world, although it be evil, conduces to the good of the universe. For, as Augustine says, God is so good that He would not permit anything evil unless He were so great as to draw something good out of every evil." However, the beneficiaries of this providence are not said to be all men, but "those who love God." As regards these, "whatever happens either to them or to other things, all turns out to their benefit . . . (so that) also the wicked actions of sinners conspire to the advantage of the just." Even their own sins are not excluded from this economy. "So far does God make all things cooperate to their gain that if any of them should deviate or stray from the right path, this also He uses to their profit . . . since the just man rises from his fall more cautious and more humble. . . . Such persons learn how fearful they must be in the midst of (spiritual) prosperity and not presume to remain faithful on the strength of their own virtue."[9]

The number and variety of external graces defy classification. As a general principle, the love of God transforms everything which is good, and not only such things as appear good to us. This includes temporal afflictions and adversities which God uses to convert and sanctify our souls. No matter how painful, they are a grace of God, always intended as such for the one suffering and sometimes used by Him for the conversion and sanctification of others. Included also are the actions of other people. Their ordinary words and conduct are intended to occasion supernatural effects in our souls. This will be hard to see where the actions are offensive or the offender is not personally wicked and may even be highly virtuous. It is of special importance to see God operating in the opposition and perhaps criminal actions of others. Yet, as seen from Scripture, He

[9] S. Thomas, *Commentaria in Epistolas S. Pauli*, Vol. I, Liége, 1857, pp. 160–161. In his treatment of the subject here and in the *Summa Theologica* (I^a II^{ae}, q. 79, a. 4; III^a, q. 89, a. 2), St. Thomas carefully refers this special supernatural providence, which derives eventual profit even from sin, to the elect, i.e., "who according to His purpose are saints through His call." He argues to their being the object of the good intended by God when permitting evil because they represent "the most noble parts" of the universe, much as "a doctor might allow the foot to be injured in order to heal the head."

permits these things in order to draw good out of them. St. Paul's eulogy on the great believers of the Old Law, Noe, Abraham, Moses, Jacob and Joseph, is an application of this principle. The Lord tries His servants by sending them trials, and their sanctification depends on the measure of faith which recognizes in these temporal obstacles the workings of divine grace, no less than in the pleasant circumstances of daily life.

Perfection of the "More": The term "more" appears in the last sentence of the autograph text of the Exercises and is generally accepted as authentic. A literal translation of the Spanish reads, ". . . solely desiring and choosing that which more leads us to the end for which we are made." Consequently, the expression "which *most* lead us to the end," as found in some English versions, gives an interpretation of the text. According to Father Nadal, "the closing phrase of the Foundation so envisions our indifference that we choose and desire those things which lead us more to attain the end of our creation."[10] It may be described as a statement of the perfection of indifference, following the doctrine of St. Thomas that: "A man's soul is so much the more perfectly drawn to God as it is more detached from affection for temporal things." This is the end product of Christian spirituality, since "all the counsels by which we are invited to perfection have this end in view: that being detached from the love of earthly goods, our souls may tend more freely to God."[11]

Besides describing the perfection of indifference, the last sentence also proposes the surest means of becoming indifferent. St. Ignatius recommends two acts of the will—desire and choice—which, if consistently applied to objects that are more conducive to the end of our existence, gradually neutralize the natural inclination we have to follow creatures without reference to their Creator. Deceptively short, it reduces to practice the main function of the evangelical counsels in the scheme of

[10] *Monumenta Historica,* "Epistolae P. Nadal," IV, Madrid, 1905, p. 835.
[11] Ia IIae, q. 108, a. 4.

salvation. By their means, says St. Thomas, a person "more freely attains to the end for which he was created."[12]

The closing words of the Foundation also clarify what indifference is not. It is not mere passivity in the presence of creatures, allowing them to pound the will with opposition, nor mere stoicism which resists their seductive attraction with no supernatural end in view. It is an active dynamism that positively seeks out those creatures which the mind, illumined by faith, determines are more conducive to the Beatific Vision. Behind this clarification stands the implicit principle that there are degrees of efficiency among creatures as instruments of sanctification, and that consequently it behooves us to train the mind for recognizing which are the more efficacious and to develop the will habitually to embrace them.

Therefore, a logical relation exists between indifference and the *tantum-quantum* rule which takes on a depth of meaning not otherwise apparent. When St. Ignatius urges us to use creatures in so far as they assist and abstain from them in so far as they hinder our salvation, the issue involved is more than obedience to precept or the avoidance of sin. It includes the delicate appraisal of every creature for its efficiency in leading us to our appointed end, and its choice or rejection should depend on the degree to which it answers to this requirement.

[12] *Ibid.*

2

Estrangement From God

T HE doctrinal background of the Spiritual Exercises is the
creature's estrangement from the Creator. In the First
Week the main theme of the meditations is sin — angelic,
original and personal — with its painful retribution in death,
judgment and hell. In the mortal life of Christ, from the Incarnation to the Passion, sin occasioned the coming of the
Redeemer who suffered and died for its expiation on the cross.
And finally in the Resurrection, we see the conquest of the
consequences of sin and the correlative promise of heaven,
"where the former things will have passed away and sin will be
no more." Thus in a true sense sin was never far from the
mind of St. Ignatius in the Exercises, as something to be recognized and feared, deplored and fought against with all the powers that grace and nature can afford.

REALIZING THE GRAVITY OF SIN

Objectively and theoretically no Christian will doubt that
sin is the worst evil in the world. One venial sin, as Newman
describes it, is more terrible in the eyes of God than the death
of millions of men in extremest agony. Yet practically sin is
so common, even among those who profess to believe in Christ
and are bound by the most solemn promises to His devoted
service.

St. Ignatius was conscious of the variance between faith and
practice and therefore early in the Spiritual Exercises placed a
series of meditations that are calculated to deepen our realiza-

14

tion of the gravity of sin. He believed this conviction was indispensable if we are to amend our lives and avoid offending God in the future.

The first and radical knowledge of the malice of sin in the Exercises derives from a consideration of its effects. The wages of sin is death: bodily death to the human race for the sin of Adam and spiritual death in hell for the unrepentant sinner. For Adam and his progeny it means the dissolution of the most intimate union under heaven, a tearing apart of matter and spirit that God Himself has ordained for mutual composition. For the demons and their victims it means the separating of a created spirit from the Source of its happiness for eternity. All this because of sin.

Characteristically the Exercises do not stress the visible or temporal effects of sin, like loss of reputation and friends, dishonor and physical distress, sickness in body and mind—no doubt because they are insignificant by comparison with the consummation of evil in hell. We also know from other writings of St. Ignatius that he looked upon physical sufferings in this world more as evidences of God's mercy seeking to convert the sinner than as signs of His justice to punish the evildoer. But one temporal effect of sin which he clearly emphasized is the Passion and Death of Christ. Ignatius makes it the first colloquy of the retreat, where he recommends that we imagine Christ before us on the cross and ask Him, "how, being our Creator, He had come to this, that He has made Himself man and from eternal life has come to temporal death." Bellarmine refers to the crucifixion as the most convincing lesson God could teach us on the malice and gravity of sin, that the Creator Himself had to become man to expiate the disobedience of His creatures.

Coming closer to the substance of sin, we get a deeper understanding of its nature by reflecting on the disproportion between the sinner and the Lord against whom he sins. Since the gravity of an insult depends on the dignity of the person insulted and his superiority to the one who commits the injury, then a deliberate flouting of the divine law, as happens in mortal sin, is the acme of wickedness. In order to bring home this infinite distance between God the offended and us the offenders, I should abase myself first by comparison with the rest of creation (a drop in the ocean of mankind), which itself is inferior to the angels and saints, who are as nothing compared with the infinite God. Then I compare myself alone with the Creator against whom I have sinned: my ignorance with His wisdom, my weakness with His omnipotence, my malice towards Him with His goodness to me.

There is more than psychology in these contrasts. They touch upon the essence of sin, which pretends to aseity or self-sufficiency, possessed by God alone but madly aspired to by every sinner since Paradise, when the devil persuaded our first parents that by eating the forbidden fruit they would become as gods, knowing good and evil. This deep-rooted instinct needs to be corrected by prayerful reflection on God's greatness and my nothingness. Otherwise past sins will scarcely be recognized as really serious and future amendment is proportionally more difficult. Especially under the stress of passion, when pressure from the senses tends to obscure the mind, I must be thoroughly convinced that because the God who obliges me to self-control is all-wise, He knows better than I what is good for me, and because He loves me more than I love myself, His commandments must be obeyed under penalty of self-destruction. Looking back, I will see how irrational my sins have been when I followed my own puny judgment in preference to the wisdom and goodness of God.

But sin is not only irrational. It is unjust. Since God is man's Creator, He has a right to determine His creatures' conduct and prescribe the conditions on which men will attain their final destiny. Not from mere habit does Ignatius constantly refer to God as the Lord. "Christ our Lord, God our Lord, Son and Lord, the Lord God, Creator and Lord, Eternal Lord" are all found (and some more than once) in the single meditation on sin to impress the retreatant with the right of dominion which God has over His creatures. The corresponding emphasis on man's dependence upon God and the consequent injustice of sin are more than ever necessary in modern times, when secularist philosophy has severed morality from religious ideals and professes a code of ethics that excludes the notion of God.

In their national pastoral of 1948, the American bishops warned against the prevalent tendency "to teach moral and spiritual values divorced from religion and based solely on social convention. Unless man's conscience is enlightened by the principles that express God's law, there can be no firm and lasting morality. Without religion, morality becomes simply a matter of individual taste, of public opinion, or majority vote."[1] Once God is removed from the concept of morals, sin becomes a label for superstition or a name for divergence from accepted custom.

Besides injustice, sin also appears as ingratitude. The sinner "acts against the Infinite Goodness" of God, to whom he owes absolutely everything, including the physical power of refusing obedience to his Creator. Ingratitude is so closely bound up with sin as practically to define it. According to St. Thomas, we are ungrateful to God when we despise the gifts received from His bounty, and sin is precisely "the contempt of God by which a man attaches himself to changeable creatures" in preference to the unchangeable Creator.[2] St. Ignatius stresses one aspect of ingratitude that is characteristic of the Exercises. A sinner contemns the divine goodness not only in the gifts of creation, but especially in the order of grace that was merited for us by the Passion and Death of Jesus Christ. Whenever we sin, therefore, we abuse more than the blessings of nature; we reject the love which raised us to the family of God.

Finally, underlying all the other phases of malice, sin deviates from the order that God established in the universe. This is the high-point of St. Ignatius' insight into the evil of sin.

---

[1] *Catholic Mind*, January 1953, p. 60.
[2] *Summa Theologica*, IIa IIae, q. 104, a. 3.

He urges the retreatant to reflect on the disorder which his perversity has introduced, so that "abhorring it, I may amend and order myself aright."

The variety of disorders that sin produces in the world is legion. Unfortunately the most serious, namely, insubordination of a creature to its Creator, may be the least obvious. More painfully evident are the corollary derangements that fill the story of every human being according to the measure of his sin: an unbridled tongue which caused a loss of reputation or grave injury to the innocent; intemperate drinking which destroyed a happy marriage and the peace of family life; unbridled passion which ruined a person's character and induced the tyranny of vice. If virtue has a law, there is also a law of sin, whose consequences are the havoc caused in the hearts and lives of countless people, beginning with the sinner and extending to everyone, though unknown and still unborn, who is in any way touched by one person's disobedience to the will of God.

ASCETICAL VALUE OF THE CONSCIOUSNESS OF SIN

Since the Spiritual Exercises are instruments of sanctification and not merely conversion, we must look for something deeper than the immediate contrition and remission of guilt as the fruit of meditation on sin. Why rehearse the sins I committed and which I trust have been forgiven? Why not look only to the future, considering how I may serve God more faithfully, and not rack my conscience with the memory of past failings? The reason is that the prospect of a life of virtue and even high sanctity is often—very often—conditioned on the abiding realization of one's sinfulness. Newman was so taken by this fact that he practically defined the Christian religion by its ability to make people conscious of their sin. Considering the actual state of man as found in this world, he said, "any standard of duty which does not convict him of real and multiplied sins, and of incapacity to please God of his own strength, is untrue; and any rule of life which leaves him contented with himself, without fear, without anxiety, without humiliation, is deceptive; it is the blind leading the blind; yet such, in one shape or another, is the religion of the whole earth, beyond the pale of the Church."[3]

The understanding of my sinfulness will make me humble, if for no other reason at least because I can scarcely pride myself on strength of character when I look back at a lifetime of weakness in resisting temptation. Pride, in the last analysis, is an over-weening self-esteem, often based on high talents or native ability. Frequently the proud man has some possession which others do not have—money, business connections, a sharp wit or social graces. Whatever it is, the more plain the disproportion between me and other people, the more likely will I be tempted to pride. But if God permitted me to sin, I am faced with the testimony of experience to discount any superiority in other things, in view of my evident failure in the most important thing in life, conforming myself to the divine will. St. Augustine, judging by his own struggle against the flesh, felt that God often brings a proud person to his senses by allowing him to fall into sins of impurity, thus humiliating his pride of intellect by exposing his surrender to temptations of the flesh.

Correlative to a deeper humility, the recognition of past sins normally leads to a distrust of self and greater reliance on God. Man is so constituted that unless he has a strong realization of his contingency, he will not easily betake himself to prayer. The spontaneous, "God help me," of otherwise unreligious people when in trouble illustrates this connection between a sense of need and asking for divine assistance. If this be true in general, it is especially true of those who aspire to perfection and higher sanctity. By profession they are not so concerned about temporal cares or even about things which stimulate most people to pray. Yet, consistent with human psychology, they will pray more earnestly as they see them-

[3] John H. Newman, "The Religion of the Pharisee, the Religion of Mankind," *Sermons on Various Occasions*, London, 1898, p. 20.

selves in definite need, which in their case is the lack of will power to resist sin, unless God supplies the grace, as past experience has proved to them.

In much the same way the recollection of past sinfulness helps to promote our charity towards the neighbor. Whenever I am tempted to criticize another person's fault, if I only reflect for a moment on my own serious sins, I place an obstacle in the way of rash judgment that is hard to overcome. No matter how I compare the evident failings of other people with my own, I can always end the comparison in their favor. Their fault may be an isolated action, by contrast with my repeated violations of the moral law; appearances are often deceiving and what externally seems to be grievously wrong, and intentionally so, on their part may be only lightly culpable or not even sinful at all, whereas I know (without guessing) the internal gravity of my own past sins. The same technique is useful for checking a tendency to depreciate the achievements or good qualities of other people by reflectively parading my own. Granted that someone is less gifted as a teacher or business man, or less popular than I. But if I balance my superiority in this area with my inferiority in the moral order, brought home to me by the consciousness of sin, the lesser advantage cancels and I am protected from uncharity when I see how irrational an invidious comparison would be.

However, the stress on sin and its consequences is not only or primarily purgative, at least in the case of exercitants who are fairly advanced in the spiritual life. St. Ignatius was mostly concerned with exciting sentiments of gratitude, where past infidelities may serve as stepping stones to future sanctity. Thus I am told to reflect on the one sin of Adam and Eve, of the angels, of a hypothetical sinner in hell, and compare this with my own many sins which may have merited eternal punishment. The climax is reached when I exclaim in wonder as I review God's creatures and ask how they have permitted me to live and sustained me. "Why the angels, who are the sword of Divine Justice, have borne with me, have guarded and prayed for me. . . . Why has the earth not opened to swallow me up, creating new hells that I might suffer in them forever."

The gratitude for God's mercy can be a powerful stimulant to make reparation for a life-time of sin. "A sinful act," says St. Thomas, "makes a man guilty of punishment to the extent to which he transgressed the order of divine justice. Nor does he restore this order except by a positive compensation, which is based on the strictest equity. Consequently the more a person has indulged his own will by disobeying a commandment of God, the order of divine justice requires that he correspondingly endure something against his will, either spontaneously or by coercion."[4] When, therefore, I see that my offenses against the Divine Majesty have not been punished "by coercion," I am moved to repay what I owe spontaneously, by voluntary expiation for my sins. I am thus motivated not only by a sense of justice to repair the divine economy I have violated, but especially by a loving generosity to compensate for past ingratitude. My sorrow for sin consequently becomes an instrument of sanctification, since the desire to amend my life is born of a conviction that whatever sacrifices this amendment may require, they are small by comparison with the suffering that my sins really deserved.

HUMAN FREEDOM AND SORROW FOR THE PAST

One aspect of St. Ignatius' treatment of sin cannot be fully appreciated except in the historical setting of the Spiritual Exercises. Ignatius stresses the power of a human will, with divine grace, to avoid sin and therefore to amend one's life for the future. If this seems like a platitude to us, it was a live issue in the sixteenth century. Among the propositions of Martin Luther condemned by the Church was the assertion that "after Adam's sin, man's free will was destroyed and lost," so that "the just man sins in every good work, and free will is a term

---

[4] *Summa Theologica*, Ia IIae, q. 87, a. 6.

without meaning; and when it does what is in its power, it sins mortally."[5]

That St. Ignatius was not oblivious of this error appears from one of his Rules for Thinking with the Church, where he expressly cautions against overemphasizing grace at the expense of human freedom. "We ought not to speak or insist on the doctrine of grace so strongly," he warns, "as to give rise to that poisonous teaching that takes away free-will."

In line with this attitude, the meditations on sin describe its intrinsic malice as arising from a perversion of created freedom. Thus "the angels were created in the state of grace, but they did not want to make use of the freedom God gave them to reverence and obey their Creator and Lord." Our first parents "sinned by violating the command not to eat of the tree of knowledge." And after reviewing my own life of sin, in colloquy with God the Father, "I will resolve with His grace to amend for the future." Always the will is conceived as perfectly free to obey or disobey, to remain in sin or be converted to God with the help of His grace.

Parallel with the stress on freedom against Protestant heresy, St. Ignatius regards contrition for sin as a "retreat" into the past and not only, as did Luther, a kind of resolution for the future. Where Ignatius has the exercitant "call to mind all the sins of my life, reviewing year by year, and period by period," in order to excite sorrow and a firm purpose of amendment, Luther held that "the kind of contrition engendered by the recollection, consideration and detestation of sins as a person reviews all his years with a bitter heart . . . this kind of contrition makes one a hypocrite, makes him, in fact, a worse sinner."[6]

The difference between Luther and Ignatius lies in their antithetical concepts of sorrow for sin. For Ignatius, contrition meant not only future amendment but also hatred of past sins because they offended God and deserved eternal punishment.

[5] Denzinger, 771, 776.
[6] *Ibid.*, 746.

For Luther, "the best penance is a new life," irrespective of any regrets for the past. Behind this notion was the implicit denial that we can be truly sorry for the wrong we have done. According to the Reformers, "it is not in man's power to make his ways evil, but God performs the evil works just as He performs the good, and not only permissively but also properly and directly, so that Judas' betrayal no less than Paul's vocation was God's own work."[7] Viewed in this atmosphere, more prevalent than ever today, the Ignatian meditations on personal sin and the fear of hell take on a more intelligible meaning. They serve to clarify a cardinal principle of Christianity, that man is a responsible agent at every stage of his moral journey through life: when he chooses evil in preference to what his conscience tells him is good; when he decides to reflect on certain motives leading to repentance for sin; when he is actually sorry for what he has done and resolves to amend his life and make reparation for his offenses against God.

By an interesting coincidence St. Ignatius was first drafting the Spiritual Exercises, with their insistence on man's responsibility, almost the very year that Luther began propagating his errors on human freedom. Ignatius made the Exercises at Manresa in the winter of 1522–1523, Luther was condemned by Leo X in 1520. When Ignatius later said that "we ought to distrust anything written by heretics," he had learned from experience how much harm can come to Catholic orthodoxy by injudicious contact with the Reformation whose theology had eliminated human liberty.

---

[7] *Ibid.*, 816.

3

The Call of Christ the King

THE contemplation on the Kingdom of Christ has been accurately called the heart of Ignatian spirituality. It epitomizes two ideals to which the exercitant is invited to aspire and which, if he follows, will bring him to "the pinnacle of perfection in the imitation of Christ." The first is a willingness to go beyond mediocrity in the service of Christ, the Son of God; the second a projection of personal love into the world outside, so that other souls may also "yield a higher than ordinary service to Christ their King."

GOSPEL ORIGINS AND PRINCIPLES

There is no speculation on where St. Ignatius got his concept of the royal invitation of Christ to His followers. All the Saviour's teaching was somehow identified with the *Basileia*, or the Kingdom, of the evangelists, from the opening of His public life when He began to preach repentance, "for the kingdom of heaven is at hand," to His dying profession before Pilate that: "My kingdom is not of this world, . . . my kingdom is not from here."[1] Christ used the word "Church" only twice to describe the society He was founding. He spoke of His "kingdom" in almost every chapter of the Gospels, so that whatever light they cast on the social aspects of Christianity must be looked for in this notion of the kingdom. If Ignatius emphasized the interior qualities of discipleship, it was only because he recognized the priority of personal dedication to

[1] Matthew 4:17; John 18:36–37.

24

anything like mass movement or communal enterprise. The
kingdom must first be implanted in the hearts of individual
Christians by their own dedicated love of the Saviour.

Two possible emphases may be placed in the contemplation
on the Kingdom, depending on the relative stress given to the
pursuit of one's own perfection or to the Christian apostolate
in its various forms. Viewed in one sense, the meditation is
directly concerned only with self-conquest and growth in holiness, and indirectly with the apostolate by generating a spirit
of zeal for the salvation of others. Viewed from a different
angle, the exercise considers both functions simultaneously: to
produce high sanctity in the imitation of Christ's virtues with
relation to God, and apostolic zeal by imitating His virtues in
the interest of mankind.[2] Perhaps the difference between the
two viewpoints is more verbal than real. But the latter approach has the advantage of not seeming to compartmentalize
the spiritual life, as though Christ could be followed on separate levels, the personal or apostolic, instead of conceiving
Christian perfection as an organic unity which seeks to imitate
the whole Saviour in the whole range of His human existence.

The ancient Directories (official manuals of instruction on
the Exercises) speak of the Kingdom as "a kind of Foundation
or Prologue of the entire treatise which follows, that is, a sum-
mary or compendium of the life and labors of Christ the Lord
in the work committed to Him by the Father."[3] It may therefore be regarded as an historical embodiment of the ideas set
forth in the first Foundation, in such a way that the main principles are now clothed in the existential context of the person
and actions of Jesus Christ. Where the Foundation considers
man in relation to God, the Kingdom places him in the presence of the God-man; and instead of limiting his gaze to his
own salvation, he is now bid to share with Christ in the redemption of others.

[2] The technical distinction is between the virtues of Christ *ad intra*, as the
Incarnate Son of God, and His virtues *ad extra*, as Redeemer of the human
race.
[3] *Monumenta Historica*, "Exercitia Spiritualia," p. 1046.

As explained by the 16th century *Apologia* of the Exercises, "St. Ignatius placed this meditation at the beginning of the Second Week as a basis for the subsequent reflections on the life of Christ in order to inspire us to imitate Him." Everyone is intended to share in this meditation: "people in the world as well as religious, those who make the election and those who do not." All must meditate on the life of Christ "with complete indifference of will to embrace the divine will and with a firm desire to attain that which is more perfect and pleasing to God. According to each person's disposition, this is accomplished by doing what is better and more in conformity with the life of Christ—whether it means the choice of a certain vocation or undertaking other good works for the greater glory of God."[4]

The imitation of Christ as proposed in the call of Christ the King forms the bedrock of the Spiritual Exercises. Actually the concept is nothing new, but goes back to the teaching of Christ, "Learn of Me . . ." and of Ignatius of Antioch, "Be imitators of Jesus Christ, as He is of the Father."[5] St. Paul exhorted the Corinthians, "Be imitators of me, as I am of Christ," and according to St. Augustine, a man is perfect if he follows Christ perfectly, while to follow perfectly is to imitate.[6] What Christian tradition had taught for centuries, St. Ignatius developed into an organic method of asceticism. Thus among the writings which most deeply influenced his spiritual outlook was the *Imitation of Christ*, where we read in the opening paragraph: "He that follows Me does not walk in darkness, says the Lord. These are the words of Christ, whereby we are admonished how we must imitate His life and conversation if we would be truly enlightened and delivered from all blindness of heart."[7]

We may legitimately ask why the imitation of Christ should

[4] *Ibid.*, pp. 694–695.
[5] St. Ignatius of Antioch, "Letter to the Philadelphians," *The Apostolic Fathers*, New York, 1947, p. 116.
[6] St. Augustine, "Sermo 142," PL 38, 783–784.
[7] *Imitation of Christ*, Book I, chap. 1.

be so essential for Christian perfection. The answer lies in the finality of the Incarnation, since this was one of the reasons why God became man, to be followed by men as a norm of sanctification. In the words of St. Augustine, "The Son of God who in the Father is ever the truth and the life, by taking upon Himself man's nature became the way. . . . By Him you are going to Him. Seek not to come to Him by any other way than Him."[8] Since mankind needed to be taught the way to God, "it had to be formed after some model. Hence the first thing necessary was that a standard and pattern of discipline be available. This was done by the divinely appointed method of the Incarnation, which is properly to be ascribed to the Son, in order that from it should follow both our knowledge, through the Son, of the Father . . . and the interior sweetness of despising all mortal creatures, which is a gift properly ascribed to the Holy Ghost."[9]

Although there are many ways that Christ can be imitated in His human nature, they may all be reduced to His practice of the virtues—mental and volitional, internal and external, personal and in relation to others. St. Ignatius gives full scope to these in detail, through the fifty meditations which form the substance of the Second and Third Weeks of the Exercises. But in the contemplation on the Kingdom he singles out one aspect of Christ as man which not only underlies the other virtues, but which synthesizes His mortal life as Redeemer of the human race. This is the aspect of Christ in the role of willing sufferer through humble obedience to the will of His heavenly Father.

With no sign of coercion, the eternal King invites us to follow Him in labor and pain, not for the sake of suffering but as the mysterious means ordained by God for the salvation of a fallen humanity. Conceived in this way, the Kingdom meditation opens a panorama of profound insights into the meaning of the cross in the economy of Redemption. A logical

8 St. Augustine, "Sermo 141," PL 38, 777.
9 St. Augustine, "Epistola XI," PL 33, 76.

relation thus arises between Christ's invitation to "follow Me in pain," and His promise, "to follow Me in glory." For if Christ is our model and the way to the Father, then the labor and suffering He underwent are a pattern for us to imitate if we wish to attain eternal happiness in His company.

SANCTITY AS THE FRUIT OF LABOR AND SUFFERING

There is also a close correlation between effort and pain as exemplified by Christ, and the sanctity to which He calls His elect. Their causal connection may be explained in terms of supernatural merit, on the basis of what elements contribute to an increase of merit in this life and a corresponding increase of glory in the life to come. Theologians commonly recognize three such factors, and subdivide the third into two parts.

According to St. Thomas, "The efficacy of merit can be measured from grace, from the will and from the object. For as an act is informed by greater charity and grace, it is to that extent more meritorious; also the more voluntary is the act, the more it has of the essence of merit and is more praiseworthy; and finally, the more arduous is an object, the higher is the merit of the act—though the comparison is always understood about one of these factors, with the others being taken as equal."[10] Applying these norms to the matter at hand, we see how naturally the following of Christ in His labor and sufferings produces greater merit in the acts of virtue thus performed.

Assuming that a person is in the state of grace, by placing an action from a motive of pure love for God, the merit he derives becomes greater than it would be if he had acted from lower motivation and with less supernatural charity.

In like manner, the greater willfulness in performing a good action, the greater liberty it indicates and the higher its merit, just as in bad actions increased advertence and freedom mean greater culpability. The imitation of Christ toiling and suffering implies a high degree of conscious deliberation and, in

[10] St. Thomas, *Super Sententiarum* II, dist. 29, q. 1, a. 4.

spite of repugnance from the lower passions, a corresponding liberty in the human will. As the action becomes not only deliberate but also joyous with untrammeled generosity, its voluntariness increases along with the merit.

Since the sublimity of an object determines the value of its corresponding act, the more noble the object of a particular virtue the greater its supernatural merit. In general, a virtue is more noble as it approaches more closely to God. Thus, *ceteris paribus*, acts of faith, hope and charity are more meritorious than those of the moral virtues. And among the former, charity is most meritorious. The faithful following of Christ, poor and humble, means the practice of the noblest virtue—love—toward its highest object—God—with no selfish interests involved. Merit in the form of grace and a title to glory is measured accordingly.

A careful distinction should be made regarding difficulty as a factor which increases merit. Much depends on the source of whatever hardship is experienced in the practice of virtue. If the source is extrinsic to the action, i.e., if it arises from culpable personal defects such as bad habits, uncontrolled passions, evil inclinations or lack of prudent vigilance, then, clearly, difficulties lower merit instead of increasing it. If, on the other hand, they are intrinsic to the action or at least not culpable in the person, the difficulties experienced add to the merit that we gain before God. Thus if the work to be done is arduous or sublime of its very nature, if its accomplishment requires overcoming severe temptations and external or even internal obstacles arising from temperament or physical conditions—then (assuming that God wishes the action to be placed) merit increases. Unlike charity and voluntariety, however, difficulty is not of the essence of merit. Yet the two are closely related either because an exalted object is difficult of attainment for being exalted, or at least "what is difficult calls for greater attention and requires greater effort of the will," so that merit increases indirectly by way of nobility of object or greater voluntariety.[11] By psychological necessity, therefore, the following of Christ in poverty and affliction gives an assurance of higher merit than the practice of virtue independently of this object and motive. Not that any merit attaches to difficulties in themselves, but because this imitation of Christ means the practice of sublimest virtue and evokes the exercise of profoundest love.

SPIRIT OF THE APOSTOLATE

The apostolic implications of the Kingdom may be inferred from the words of Christ inviting His followers to join in the enterprise of conquering the whole world for His Father at the cost of much suffering and labor. But more radically it appears from the whole purpose of Christ's life upon earth, which was to save souls. Consequently if we are to follow Christ faithfully, our purpose must be the same as His, namely, not only to develop His Kingdom in ourselves but also cooperate with divine grace to establish the same in others. On the last day, the just will be called to possess the Kingdom because they had loved Christ in His members by serving their bodily and spiritual needs. Another name for the practice of these works of mercy is the Christian apostolate—at once a condition of salvation and an opportunity for practicing the highest virtue in imitation of Christ who went about doing good for others even to the death of the cross. We may ask, when did Christ perform the most arduous labors and suffer the greatest pain if not in the years of His public life, when preaching the Gospel to an evil generation, and in the days of His passion, which crowned His apostolate as "the cause of our reconciliation with God"?[12] Our own labor and pain, therefore, in union with Christ the Redeemer are also joined to the apostolate, and can no more be separated from the following of Christ than His sufferings can be divorced from His role as the Saviour of mankind.

[11] *Ibid.*
[12] St. Thomas, *Summa Theologica*, IIIa, q. 49, a. 4.

It is not easily apparent why Christ should invite us to imitate His practice of poverty and suffering in order to conquer the world for the glory of His Father. Why not directly invite His followers to join in proclaiming the word of God to the ends of the earth? Why this preoccupation with personal sanctification and the emphasis on mortification of carnal and worldly love? The reason is two-fold: one based on the nature of man and the character of the apostolate, and the other derived from the providence of God in the order of grace and the supernatural.

Without invoking any authority, common experience teaches that successful work for souls, in whatever form, requires the practice of the moral virtues in a high degree. There is need for patience in bearing with weakness and ignorance in oneself and others; courage to surmount difficulties arising from one's own temperament, from opposition, or natural circumstances; industry in willingness to sacrifice comfort and ease for the benefit of others; self-control in restraining disordinate affections and repressing unreasonable fears. Without these virtues it is quite impossible to convert people from a life of sin or lead them to spiritual perfection. If nothing else, they need our example to know that what we ask them to do is not impossible and worth the effort of striving for.

But the apostolate is not only a work of nature. It is preeminently in the realm of grace, where supernatural help in the form of light and strength and infusion of faith, hope and charity are the direct operation of the Holy Spirit. Here especially must be sanctity in the human instrument to cooperate successfully with God for the sanctification of others. "To one who wishes to qualify himself for apostolic work," said Benedict XV, "there is one thing he must acquire before everything else, as being of the highest importance, it is . . . sanctity of life. Let him therefore be an example of humility, obedience, chastity, chiefly of piety, prayer and constant union with God. The better united he is with God, the greater will be his share of divine grace and assistance. Let him heed the Apostle's counsel, 'Put on, therefore, as God's chosen ones, holy and beloved, a heart of mercy, kindness, humility, meekness, patience' (Col. 3:12). It is by these virtues that truth finds an easy and straight access to souls, and that all obstacles are removed. There is no obstinacy of will that can resist them."[13] According to St. Vincent de Paul, "We must hold it as an infallible axiom that in proportion as we labor for our inward perfection, we enable ourselves the more to bear fruit for our neighbor."[14]

St. Ignatius explains the relation between holiness and the apostolate by analogy with natural causes:

The law which God has made to govern the process of generation in the natural order, obtains, proportionately, in the supernatural order as well. Philosophy and what we see around us go to show that, besides the general or universal causes, such as the elements, a special and immediate cause of the same species is further needed, in order that the animal or man produced be of like kind with the agent producing. In the same way, therefore, it is the will of Divine Wisdom that the immediate cause employed, such as the preacher or confessor, be himself humble, patient and filled with charity. Consequently, if you would perfect others, be perfect yourselves first. For though great learning and great virtue are to be sought after, and perfection looked for in both, yet virtue must always be given the preference.[15]

Theologically, the influence of personal sanctity on the apostolate may be described in terms of supernatural merit. It is common teaching in the Church that a person in God's friendship can truly, though not in strict justice, merit actual and sanctifying grace for others. The Scriptures often stress the need for this spiritual altruism. . . . "pray for one another," St. James urges, "that you may be saved. For the unceasing prayer of a just man is of great avail" (James 5:16). In the

13 Benedict XV, Apostolic Letter *Maximum Illud*, November 30, 1919, *Acta Apostolicae Sedis*, Vol. 11, pp. 449–450.
14 St. Vincent de Paul (Complete Works), Paris, 1920–1925, Vol. XI, p. 28.
15 *Monumenta Historica*, "Monumenta Ignatiana," Series 1, Tomus 1 (Letter dated May 7, 1547), Madrid, 1903, pp. 508–590.

Christian apostolate, this prayer may be explicit as petition or implicit in the labors and efforts undergone for the salvation of souls. However, what is most significant for our purpose, its efficacy in the form of grace obtained for others is the merit-value it has in the eyes of God. And all the norms which regulate the increase of merit in general are equally valid here. As an apostle's charity becomes more ardent, his freedom less impeded by inordinate attachments, his object less selfish and more noble, in a word, the more holy he is, the more efficacious becomes his prayer of action and petition to obtain grace for those in whose interest he labors.

We may therefore look upon the Kingdom meditation as a call to follow Christ in the conquest of our carnal and worldly desires; the more generous the effort the more closely we approach to His own divine perfection and become daily more eligible for the glory that awaits us in His company. At the same time, in the very act of following the Master through self-conquest, we are cultivating those virtues which advance the kingdom of God on earth and increase its population in heaven. As members of the Mystical Body, our union with Christ is itself a petition for divine mercy for those in need; and among the instruments of the apostolate none is more effective than prayer and sacrifice offered with the Redeemer on behalf of souls.

4

The Standards of Christ and Lucifer

COMMENTATORS are agreed that this is one of the "great" meditations of the Exercises, as evident from the elaborate detail of its composition and from the reference to its importance in other writings of St. Ignatius. It is also unique in having what may be called two corollaries: the Three Classes of Men and the Three Modes of Humility, where the basic principles of the Two Standards are further specified and applied to the exercitant's immediate needs.

Apart from its intrinsic ascetical value, the meditation on the Two Standards crystallizes the ideals of the Christian apostolate introduced by the call of Christ the King. One of its principal conclusions, therefore, describes the following of Christ as a social and apostolic venture, where a dedicated soul goes beyond the desire for its own sanctification to cooperate with Christ "in propagating His doctrine among all men throughout the world."

In the Spanish autograph, this meditation is entitled, *De Dos Banderas*, without the definite article (*las*) which might have implied that the whole world must be ranged under one or the other leader. More specifically, St. Ignatius envisions those who are most active and prominent in the respective camps of Christ and Satan, although the Two Standards may be proposed even to those who are not going on to make the Election.

The purpose of this meditation is to help dispose the exercitant to make a good election on his state of life, or, if that is fixed, on its more perfect fulfillment in the following of Christ. In the words of St. Ignatius, by means of this exercise we are to "consider the intention of Christ our Lord, and on the other side that of the enemy of our human nature, and how we ought to dispose ourselves in order to arrive at perfection in whatever state or kind of life God shall give us to choose." It is the first in a triad of such predisposing exercises, along with the Three Classes of Men and the Three Modes of Humility.

There is an advance in the Two Standards over the meditation on Kingdom in several ways:

Where the Kingdom represents a simple call to follow Christ, the Two Standards points up the existence of another and contrary call from the enemy of Christ, Satan, to follow him.

In the Kingdom, the difficulties to be experienced in following Christ are either inherent in human nature or at least not created by opposition from a malicious will; but in the Standards the origin of the conflict is the hatred of the devil against Christ and His faithful servants.

The call of Christ the King is to imitate Him, "in bearing all insults and reproaches and all poverty,"—but without further explanation or motivation. In the Standards these are supplied, where poverty is shown to be the normal source of reproaches, which are the means to humility, the basis of all other virtues.

Although the call to the apostolate was implicit in the Kingdom, it is explicit and of the essence of the Two Standards, where Christ "the Lord of the whole world chooses out so many persons, apostles and disciples, and sends them throughout the whole world diffusing His sacred doctrine through all states and conditions of men."

DIABOLICAL TEMPTATIONS

It is a matter of faith that by God's permissive will the devils try to lead men into sin. Temptations come from the devils' malice. "Out of envy they try to impede man's progress, and out of pride they seek to usurp the power of God, deputing certain ministers to contend against men, just as the angels of God minister in definite offices for the salvation of men."[1]

However, not all temptations come directly from the devil. Indirectly, no doubt, Satan incited Adam to sin and by his fall induced into human nature a certain proneness to evil. In that sense the devil may be called the source of all temptation and sin. But concretely and immediately, sin proceeds not only from the devil but also from concupiscence and the misuse of our liberty. "Even if there were no devil," says St. Thomas, "men would have a desire for food, venereal pleasure and the like. Especially because of fallen nature, a great deal of de-ordination follows in this area unless the appetites are controlled by right reason; but the final restraint and proper ordination of these appetites depends on the free will. Consequently it is not necessary that all sins come from the instigation of the devil, although when they do come from him, men are deceived into giving consent by the same allurement as seduced our first parents."[2]

We may legitimately ask why St. Ignatius makes no mention of concupiscence in the meditation on the Two Standards. For one thing, it would have been outside the scope of this particular exercise and not congruent with the dispositions that an exercitant should have at this stage of the retreat. The supposition is that already in the First Week, he was moved by fear of the consequences of lust and pride to resolve never again to fall into sin; furthermore it is assumed that he wishes not only to keep the commandments but also to follow the evangelical counsels; and lastly, he is supposed to be ready to embrace the fulness of Christian perfection, if God calls him to that manner of life. Given this kind of man, Ignatius wants to prepare him to hear and follow the divine vocation by re-

[1] St. Thomas, *Summa Theologica*, I^a, q. 114, a. 1.
[2] *Ibid.*, a. 3.

moving what he considers the main obstacles that stand in the way, namely, a congenital inclination towards worldly possessions and vain honors, which the devil will surely exploit to the detriment of further progress in virtue if not to the complete abandonment of God.

If at this stage the devil tempted a person to gross immorality or manifest pride, he would probably fail. So he concentrates on that form of concupiscence which the man has likely not considered. Masking himself as an angel of light, he tries to lead magnanimous souls astray by confirming their attachment to earthly goods, ostensibly for good ends, in order to nourish their desire for human praise, which leads to pride and all kinds of sin.

Another logical question is whether the diabolical strategy follows the same pattern: riches, honor to pride. St. Ignatius answers in the negative, where he qualifies the universality of this plan by saying "as he (the devil) is wont to do in most cases." This is a marginal note made by the saint himself in the Spanish autograph, which is put in parentheses in English translations.

The essential point, however, never varies in the devil's method. Its basic subtlety consists in exciting a man's desire to obtain or retain things which are indifferent in themselves, such as riches and honors, but whose desire is never without danger and not seldom actually deadly. Anyone in whatever state of life who allows himself to be thus implicated will soon experience the attacks of Satan in the form of anxiety, darkness, disturbance of mind, confusion and positive horror, calculated to drive him out of the state of perfection or at least to make perfection impossible in whatever state he is living. For this reason, riches and honors are properly denominated by St. Ignatius as nets and chains. Lucifer will picture deceptive and perishing goods as though they were real. And although it is not in his power either to give or expedite their acquisition, the devil stimulates cupidity to the point where men persuade themselves that what they ardently desire will surely be acquired, if only they persevere in the effort.[3]

PRIDE AS THE SOURCE OF ALL SIN

When St. Ignatius says that the devil leads his followers from pride to all other vices, he merely echoes the words of Scripture that "Pride is the beginning of all sin" (Ecclesiasticus 10:15). There is an obvious difficulty, however, in reconciling this with another text where St. Paul says that "The desire for money (or avarice) is the root of all evil" (I Timothy 6:10). Evidently both statements are true, but they need careful distinction, beyond the fact that St. Ignatius himself recognizes that riches lead, through honor, to pride, and thus to every kind of sin.

"Covetousness," according to St. Thomas, "as denoting a special sin, is called the root of all sins, in likeness to the root of a tree to which it furnishes the sustenance. For we see that by riches man acquires the means of committing any sin whatever, and of sating his desire for any kind of sin, since money helps him to obtain all manner of temporal goods . . . so that in this sense, desire for riches is the root of all sins."[4] It may be conceded that avarice is sometimes rooted in other evil inclinations, such as gluttony or ambition. But generally speaking the hankering for temporal possessions gives rise to other sins, and not vice versa.

Defining pride as the inordinate desire to excel, St. Thomas explains in what sense pride is the beginning of every sin:

In voluntary actions, such as sins, there is a two-fold order, of intention and of execution. In the order of intention, the basis of action is the end (or purpose in view). Now man's purpose in acquiring temporal goods is that, through their means, he may have some perfection and excellence. Therefore, from this aspect, pride, which is the desire to excel, is said to be the *beginning* of every sin. On the other hand, in the order of execution, the first place

---

[3] *Opera Spiritualia* Joannis P. Roothaan, Vol. II, p. 103.
[4] *Summa Theologica*, Iᵃ IIᵃᵉ, q. 84, a. 1.

belongs to that which by furnishing the opportunity of fulfilling all desires of sin, has the character of a root, and such are riches; so that from this point of view, avarice is the *root* of all evils.[5]

Following the above explanation, pride is the beginning of all sin because it means the spirit of self-exaltation which induces disobedience. In so far as a man is proud, he will not submit his mind and will to others, even to God; he becomes a law unto himself. Such autonomy is incompatible with obedience to the law of God, and becomes the basic disposition from which every sin must flow as from a fountain; being that insubordination of creature to Creator which takes on a variety of forms—or specific sins—according to the different circumstances in which a person finds himself.

Pride can be the origin of sin in still another sense, as described in the writings of the Fathers. It corrupts everything it touches. St. Gregory the Great explains that other sins assail those virtues only by which they themselves are destroyed: as anger destroys patience, gluttony abstinence and lust continence. But pride is not satisfied with uprooting one virtue; it is a ravaging disease which corrupts the whole spiritual life. No matter what action is placed, if motivated by pride, the end desired is vainglory and not the glory of God. "For when pride assaults the mind a kind of tyrant invests a besieged city; and the more gifted his victim, the more harshly does he rise up in authority." Once a man allows this tyranny to enter his mind, "the eye of his heart becomes closed and he loses all balance of judgment. While the good things that others do are displeasing to him, what he does, though amiss, meets with his approval. . . . Convinced that he surpasses others in everything, he walks with himself in imagination, silently chanting his own praises."[6]

Finally pride is the beginning of sin because it deprives a man of supernatural help from God, without which the as-

---

[5] *Ibid.*, a. 2.
[6] St. Gregory I, "Liber Moralium," xxxiv, PL 76, 744–745.

saults of temptation cannot be overcome. "God resists the proud" (I Peter 5:5). On his part, the proud man does not ask for divine grace, and therefore does not receive what would have been given to him in answer to humble prayer; on the part of God, the Lord will not force His assistance on a will that refuses to cooperate.

Also to be noted is that when St. Ignatius speaks of riches as leading to pride, the riches may be either material or spiritual:

> One person prides himself on gold, another on the highest and heavenly virtues. And yet one and the same thing is going on before the eyes of God, though, as it comes to the hearts of men, it is clothed in their sight with a different garb. At first a man may have been proud of some earthly possession, and later on is elated at his sanctity; in either case, it is still the same pride which has only changed appearances in order not to be recognized.[7]

Spiritual pride, of talent or virtue, is especially possible in persons who have risen above material and secular interests; hence the besetting temptation against which consecrated souls in the cloister and the active apostolate should be warned.

Comparable to pride as the source of all evil, humility is the fountainhead of all virtue. Properly speaking, "humility is the reverence by which a man subjects himself to God."[8] As the disposition of will which inclines a man to subordinate himself to the divine will, it is fundamental to the practice of any virtue. It is also the *conditio sine qua non* for obtaining and profiting from the grace of God. In this sense especially, "humility holds the first place" among the virtues. "It drives out pride, which God resists; it makes a man submissive and always ready to receive the influx of divine grace." So that "humility is said to be the foundation of the spiritual edifice" as its indispensable condition.[9]

[7] *Ibid.*
[8] *Summa Theologica*, II[a] II[ae], q. 161, a. 3.
[9] *Ibid.*

This is the meaning of the classic passages in patristic litera-ture on the importance of humility in the spiritual life, follow-ing the teaching of Christ who bade us imitate Him above all in the practice of this virtue. St. Augustine says that the whole life of Christ on earth was a lesson in humility, which explains its relation to the other virtues. "The reason why Christ par-ticularly commended humility to us was because thereby is removed the chief obstacle to man's salvation. For man's salvation consists in tending to things heavenly and spiritual, from which he is hindered by striving to magnify himself in earthly things. For the removal of this obstacle, therefore, our Lord has shown by examples of humility how external great-ness should be despised. Thus humility is a predisposition to man's free approach to spiritual and divine blessings."[10]

In relation to supernatural perfection, humility serves the function of clearing the way. The negative hindrance that must absolutely be removed is pride, which repels God and which God repels. By removing this elementary barrier to the influx of grace, humility is properly considered the source of whatever virtue is acquired in the supernatural life. When revelation tells us that "God resists the proud, but gives grace to the humble" (James 4:6), this is not only a statement of God's economy—the more humility the more grace—but a law of human liberty in cooperation (or conflict) with divine generosity, that unless a man is humble he will (in the measure of his pride) resist whatever grace he receives.

CALL TO A SPECIAL APOSTOLATE

Analysts of the Spiritual Exercises see in the meditation on the Two Standards the "social moment" in the following of Christ by active cooperation with Him in the salvation of souls. "Everything else is subordinated to this new ideal of service. The service of the Divine Majesty becomes synony-

---

[10] *Ibid.*, a. 5.

mous with the helping of souls, which is work to be done within the Church Militant."[11]

The most concise statement of the apostolate in the Exercises occurs in this meditation. Parallel readings of the autograph and original Latin or vulgate version will supply certain details not found in English translations generally based on the Spanish:

Spanish Autograph	Vulgate Version
Consider how the Lord of all the world chooses so many persons, apostles, disciples, etc., and sends them throughout the whole world to spread His sacred doctrine among all men, no matter what their state or condition.	Closely examine how the Lord of all creation personally sends forth chosen apostles, disciples and other ministers throughout the world, to impart to every race, class and condition of mankind His sacred and salvific doctrine.

This statement of principle deserves to be more fully analyzed since it contains all the essentials of Catholic evangelism.

The one represented as sending men and women into the apostolate is "the Lord of all creation," yet God in human form, who is Jesus Christ. During His life on earth, Christ sent the apostles and disciples by a personal commission from Himself; since the Ascension, this commission still ultimately comes from Christ, but immediately through His Vicar on earth, the Roman Pontiff. Consequently the only valid basis for the apostolate is to be sent (*apostellein*) by God through His authentic representatives to a definite work for souls.

But not everybody is sent, since "the Lord chooses," and the ones sent are "chosen." No matter how large the absolute number, they are still only a fraction of all the faithful. The principle of choice is a mystery hidden in God. Yet one of the signs for this grace of vocation is precisely the ideals of this meditation generously accepted and followed through to their logical conclusion. If I have the willingness, born of grace, to

[11] Ignacio Iparraguirre, *A Key to the Study of the Spiritual Exercises*, Calcutta, 1955, p. 68.

follow Christ in poverty and humility for the conquest of souls, then I have a call to the apostolate, whatever its concrete form may be, as elaborated in the Three Classes, the Three Modes and the retreat Election. A retreatant may well have an apostolic vocation in the true sense, without being necessarily called to the priesthood or the religious life, since, in the formula of Pius XI "The call to the laity to participate in the hierarchical apostolate constitutes a vocation truly and properly so called."[12]

Christ sends His disciples "throughout the whole world," according to the universality of the apostolic commission "to preach the Gospel to every creature." Hence the responsibility for the truly apostolic spirit to be willing to work anywhere for the salvation of souls, since the desire of Christ is so manifest. He wants *all* men to be saved. Where an apostle's scope of labor is limited, he yet strains to be as widely effective as possible, never complacently satisfied that he has reached the limit of his influence. The phrase, "every class and condition," is typically Ignatian in stressing the need of bringing the Gospel to every level of society, and not only to the wealthy or externally cultured. The admonition goes back to apostolic times, when St. James had to warn the early Christians, "Do not join faith in our glorious Lord Jesus Christ to partiality towards persons. . . . Has not God chosen the poor of this world to be rich in faith and heirs of the Kingdom?" (James 2:1, 5).

The directives from Christ are to spread or impart His sacred and saving doctrine to all mankind. Again a paraphrase on the Gospels, "Going therefore teach all nations . . . teaching them to observe whatsoever I have commanded you." The immediate purpose of the apostolate is to transmit the truths of revelation since, in the providence of God, "faith comes by hearing," which means that someone who has the faith zealously passes it on to others. The measure of his zeal will be the

[12] Pius XI, Address to the Directors of the Roman Catholic Action, April 19, 1931, in Luigi Civardi, *Manual of Catholic Action*, 1943, p. 56.

depth of his conviction that faith is essentially a social possession, to be acquired only from other human beings, and
conserved also only by their instruction, ministry, prayer and
example. St. Ignatius' accent on imparting "sacred doctrine"
illustrates his characteristic insistence on the intellectual foundation of all solid conversion, up to the perfect service of
evangelical obedience, where the human mind submits to the
mind of an earthly superior, vested with the authority of God.

5

Three Classes of Men

THE title, *Three Classes of Men*, stands for three kinds of persons in any walk of life. They might be three classes of religious or priests, husbands or wives, workers or professional men. However classified, they represent three levels of volitional disposition to sacrifice whatever is less than God and stands in the way of His more perfect service and love. Viewed from another aspect, they are three states of spiritual detachment which in ascending degree dispose a man for the reception of divine grace. Implicit in the meditation is the belief that no matter how entangled in secular pursuits and impeded in the way of perfection, a person can rise above this condition if he takes the trouble to recognize these impediments and is humble enough to pray for help to overcome them.

Meditation on the Three Classes is the second stage in the soul's preparation for the Election. In relation to the Two Standards it brings the battle between Christ and Satan out of the realm of theory into practical, everyday life. What the Two Standards teach objectively about the cosmic struggle of Satan against Christ, the Three Classes depict psychologically, in the mind and will of the exercitant. Also a new element enters in the conflict between flesh and spirit, or nature and grace, as described by St. Paul: "The flesh lusts against the spirit, and the spirit against the flesh; for these are opposed to each other, so that you do not do what you would" (Galatians 5:17).

St. Ignatius describes three classes of persons, all presumably past the Principle and Foundation, who want to know and

45

achieve what is more pleasing to God. But they are laboring under the difficulty of an inordinate affection for some creature, typified by a large sum of money. The three groups have one thing in common, the same sort of creature with the same kind of effect on the will, an unreasonable affection for the object possessed. They are also alike in wanting to be rid of the inordinate affection, but they differ in the means required for getting rid of the attachment.

One class only want to be rid of the attachment, and are unwilling to use any means to that effect. They fail in the fundamental prudence which demands that suitable means be taken to attain a given end. A variety of reasons may account for this velleity: it may be sloth which avoids the effort necessary to remove the obstacles; or avarice which dreads to make a sacrifice of some long-cherished possession; or fear which shrinks from losing an apparently harmless bodily comfort or spiritual consolation; or lack of self-confidence about meeting and overcoming the difficulties; or want of conviction on the importance of becoming internally detached and a certain impracticality on the method to use; or finally a weak faith which distrusts the mercy of God to supply all the graces necessary "to find God our Lord in peace" of mind and heart.

The second class will compromise: they want to be rid of the internal impediment and also retain the external possession. They want to shape the course of providence to suit themselves, instead of adapting themselves to the demands of providence. Evidently not all creatures we possess make us inordinately attached to them. The cumulative factors which produce attachment are manifold and frequently beyond our control—assuming that the creature itself is retained. It may well be that a given object, like money, a position or favorite pastime of which I am now enamored, may be kept or continued without sacrificing the object and detachment achieved. But if I am sincere in wanting to be freed of a psychological burden, I must be willing to dispose of the physical entity which causes the unruly interior effect; otherwise when the time comes (if it comes) to sacrifice what I possess, I will not do so even though I know full well there is no other way of deliverance from the attachment.

The third class have the generosity to dispose of the creature (outside themselves) if this is necessary to shake off a dangerous affection (within themselves). They apply without hesitation the basic norms of the Principle and Foundation: the *tantum quantum* rule which measures the use or abstinence from creatures only by their utility to attain the end of man's creation; and the rule of the counsels, which is not satisfied with a minimal service of God, but wants to do whatever is more conducive to salvation and more pleasing to the Divine Majesty.

SELF-LOVE AND DETACHMENT

Assuming that the object I possess is not intrinsically sinful, I can still be unduly attached to it, as may be recognized by certain signs. Some of these are external and others can only be experienced internally.

If the object occupies my mind at times that should be free of such pre-occupation, like prayer or necessary duties; or if the amount of attention I give to the person, place, or thing is out of proportion to its objective value and importance. The standard hierarchy of values: supernatural, spiritual, intellectual and material may be applied here. So that if, for example, I am more concerned with an intellectual project than with my spiritual obligations to the evident detriment of the latter, I ought to suspect undue affection for the former.

If I find myself habitually taking complacence in some possession, to the point where I tend to contemn or pity others for lacking what I have, this is a sign of inordinate self-love.

If I often lose peace of mind from definable or undefinable causes, on account of what I have or do, I am too attached to the object, person or practice, since ordinate affection, being orderly, produces tranquillity of mind which is the essence of peace.

If I am always afraid of losing or being hindered in the use of some gift or possession, or if I feel dissatisfied with what I have, whether its amount, quality or perfection, I am too enamored of the object because the right kind of affection precludes such anxiety.

If I regularly talk about my achievement along certain lines or advertise what I have for no better reason than the pleasure I get from being recognized, this is a sign of disorder in the appetitive faculties.

If I am inclined to envy others for some kind of talent, production, or property which I feel outshines or obscures my own, this is a danger signal pointing to the need for greater self-control.

If I tend to be jealous of what I have, slow to share it with others or fearful that others may acquire the same, I am overly in love with the creature, no matter how lawfully acquired or how holy the thing may be in itself.

St. Ignatius states without analysis that the test of true detachment is to be willing either to keep or put away a creature to which a person has become strongly attracted. Why, we ask, should this be so? Why is it necessary to be ready physically to relinquish something—wealth, employment, a mode of action—as a guarantee that I am detached from the creature in question? Why is it not sufficient, as in the second class of men, "to remove the attachment (psychologically), yet so wish to remove it as to remain (physically united) with the thing acquired"? The reason lies deep in the psychology of Christian asceticism.

Any creature I possess outside of my own mind and will, and to which I am strongly attached, carries with it beneficial effects which I enjoy when and in so far as the creature is used. Money is a ready example; less obvious but equally pertinent are cultural possessions or even spiritual things in the intellectual and moral order, like methods of teaching or business, preaching and prayer, or certain opinions, religious or secular, in the practical or theoretical sphere. My will may become more or less bound to any of these because I have learned from experience what comfort, pleasure and joy they afford me when I use them. But when on reflection I discover that my attachment is inordinate, I am faced with the decision of either compromising or going "all out" in ridding myself of the disorderly affection. St. Ignatius would have it that unless I am ready to be rid of the *thing itself*, I am not really sincere in the desire to correct the malaffection. Why so?

Whenever a creature produces an undue attraction, the fault or defect must not be sought in the object as such, but rather in me. Evidently, because the same creature may be safely possessed by someone else without detriment or even with positive benefit to his spiritual life. Perhaps I have not received the grace necessary both to keep physically and spiritually to profit from the disturbing creature. Or I may be lacking, culpably or otherwise, in those qualities of mind and temperament needed to overcome the natural seductiveness of what disturbs my peace of mind. Or most certainly, the state of life to which God has called me makes demands on my generosity and self-sacrifice which cannot be properly fulfilled except at the cost of being freed of certain inordinate affections. In any case, there is no objective assurance of becoming volitionally detached unless I remove what stimulates the attachment, namely, the object itself. There is a limit to my ability to be exposed to the stimulus and to remain ordinately attached. And even this limit is unpredictable, undefinable and uncertain. To make sure I am delivered of a troublesome affection, I must remove its stimulating source. The degree of my readiness to do this determines my sincerity.

TWO KINDS OF INORDINATE AFFECTION

Besides looking at inordinate affections psychologically, as above, they can be studied entitatively, in terms of the end from which they deflect. In general, the end in view is the love

and service of God, manifested in obedience to the commandments or observance of the counsels. The radical obstacles to
achieving this end are the inordinate affections we have for
creatures, which prevent or hinder our love of God. There is a
difference, however, between overcoming inordinate affections
that stand in the way of loving God through precepts, and removing those which impede loving Him through the counsels.
The former are mandatory and binding in conscience under
grave or venial sin; the latter are not of themselves obligatory,
but offer opportunities for showing extraordinary love and ren-
dering signal service to the Divine Majesty.

St. Ignatius directs the meditation on the Three Classes
immediately to correcting whatever affections hinder the observance of the counsels, whether to be undertaken for the
first time or already embraced as a permanent mode of life. A
careful distinction should therefore be made between the two
meanings that "counsel" has in ascetical literature.

Counsel may refer to the practice of the theological virtue
of charity beyond what is prescribed under pain of sin. The accent is on the word "practice," because we are always bound to
intend to love God as perfectly as possible, following the injunction of Christ, "Thou shalt love the Lord thy God with
thy whole heart." But we are not obliged always to exercise
the most perfect kind of love in practice. Thus, for example,
to renew acts of divine love every hour is in itself more perfect
than to make them only once a day; but there is no strict
obligation to do so. The same can be said of any virtue commanded by the love of God. I may never intend to set a limit
on the intensity to which my good actions are animated by
theological charity, but I am not required always to place the
most exalted possible degree of these virtues. Accordingly, St.
Thomas clearly distinguishes between two modes or degrees of
adherence to God in charity. "One is necessary for salvation,
to which all men are obliged, i.e., that our hearts be not attached to anything which is contrary to God but are habitually

referred to Him. The other is the way of supererogation when a person adheres to God beyond the common state."[1]

More generally, counsels refer to the moral virtues which are practiced beyond their strict necessity to keep out of sin, as means of attaining the love of God in which Christian perfection essentially consists. They are consequently instruments of perfection which facilitate the acquisition of divine charity and increase its supernatural intensity. Speaking of adherence to God by way of supererogaton, St. Thomas explains that "this takes place by detaching the heart from temporal things, and thus more clearly approximating heavenly glory, since the more cupidity decreases, charity is increased."[2]

The two kinds of counsel are intimately connected, as means are related to end. By detachment from creatures in the spirit of the third class of men, we become better disposed to practice the love of God and neighbor, and more fit to make acts of charity of greater merit in the eyes of God. Traditionally the word "counsel" has become associated with an above average practice of certain moral virtues, notably poverty, chastity and obedience, as useful media for growing in theological charity. In this sense, we may say that perfection consists secondarily and instrumentally in the counsels. In fact, all the counsels, like the precepts, are directed to promote charity, but in a different way. The precepts other than the two commandments of love are intended to remove whatever is contrary to this virtue, whatever might destroy it. But the counsels are ordained to remove the impediments to the practice of charity, even though not directly opposed to it, such as marriage, preoccupation with business and civil responsibilities.[3] While precepts and counsels, therefore, both subserve charity, the one in indispensable, the other only helpful. Observance of the precepts (excluding the precepts of love) elimi-

---

[1] St. Thomas, "In Epist. ad Philippenses," cap. 3, *Opera Omnia*, Vol. XIII (Parma Edition), New York, 1949, p. 522.

[2] *Ibid.*

[3] *Summa Theologica*, IIa IIae, q. 184, a. 3.

nates only what directly opposes charity, whereas the counsels remove whatever may hinder its positive practice.

We should add, however, that the counsels (in the second sense) have still another function, namely, to contribute to the actual perfection of charity—which is more than removing impediments to its exercise. "Fasts, vigils, meditation on Holy Scripture, disposal and deprivation of all one's possessions do not constitute perfection. They are instruments of perfection. It is not in them that the science of perfection consists, but through them that the end of this science is achieved. Consequently we depend on these steps to reach the perfection of charity."[4]

In the spirit of the third class, as a person faithfully lives out the evangelical counsels he facilitates the practice of charity by removing obstacles that stand in the way. Thus a religious is freed from the burden of material possession through poverty, of family care and worry through chastity, and of personal independence through obedience. But more than facilitating the practice of charity towards God and neighbor, the counsels add to its intrinsic perfection through additional grace which their practice obtains and the numerous occasions they offer to exercise the most selfless love of God.

A word of clarification may be added on the practical correlation between the precepts and counsels. According to the common doctrine, it would be misleading to say that the Christian life as such consists in obeying the commandments, and perfection in observing the counsels. Perfection means obedience to the precepts and keeping a certain number of counsels. After proving that perfection is nothing else than the love of God and neighbor, St. Thomas explains that in practice it consists *essentially* in the commandments (especially charity) and *secondarily* in the counsels, whose function is to remove the obstacles that hinder the exercise of charity.

[4] *Ibid.* Confer Cassian's *De Monachi Intentione ac Fine*, Collatio I, PL 49, 490.

Two points should be emphasized. First the indispensability of observing the commandments of God and the Church in the quest for perfection, and not neglecting these in favor of works of supererogation. Without the precepts, perfection lacks the necessary foundation. And secondly, the need of practicing the counsels, at least some of them and at least by internal disposition, like the spirit of poverty and chastity for people in the world. Without some of the counsels (practiced according to one's state of life, the inspiration of grace and the advice of a spiritual director), perfection is impeded by unruly attachments and lacks the scope for generosity which it naturally desires.

6

Modes of Humility

THE expression "Degrees of Humility" does not occur in either the Spanish autograph or the recognized versions of the original text. The Spanish uses the term *maneras* or types of humility; the various Latin translations use Species or Modes. There is more than subtilty behind these synonyms. By definition, degree implies a quantitative difference, whereas mode and species are qualitative. Accordingly, the second mode differs from the first, and the third from the first two, not only in having more humility but in being humility of a qualitatively higher kind. In other words, to rise from a lower to a higher type of humility (in the Ignatian sense) means not merely to accumulate more of what we already possess, but to enter into an essentially superior form of moral disposition. Since the term "Degrees of Humility" is commonly acceptable, there is no problem in using it; as there is also some advantage in knowing the proper meaning which the Exercises attach to this name.

ASCETICAL THEME

The purpose of the meditation on the Three Modes of Humility is still better to prepare the exercitant for a good Election. By contrast with the Three Classes, the Modes represent the last preparatory stage before the actual Election. Where the function of the Classes was primarily negative, to remove inordinate affection for creatures, the Modes are strictly positive, to test and inspire the will for complete dedication to the service of God. In the words of St. Ignatius, "Before any one enters on the Election, that he may be *well affected* towards the teaching of Christ our Lord, it will be profitable to consider and examine the following modes of humility."

As conceived by the Exercises, humility is the proper disposition that a human will should assume in relation to the divine, and may reach one of three levels of union with the will of God, in ascending order of sublimity.

The first type of humility means that quality of submission to the Divine Majesty which makes the will ready to sacrifice any created good, even life itself, rather than disobey a commandment of God binding under mortal sin. In terms of indifference, it requires habitual detachment at least from those creatures which may not be enjoyed without loss of sanctifying grace.

The second type of humility is essentially higher. It presupposes the first and goes beyond it with a readiness to sacrifice anything rather than offend God by venial sin. Like the first, it also requires detachment from creatures, and not only from those which are sinful but to a certain extent also from such as may legitimately be used without sin. To practice the second mode, I should be no more "inclined to have riches rather than poverty, to seek honor rather than dishonor, to desire a long life rather than a short life, provided in either alternative I would promote equally the service of God and the salvation of my soul." St. Ignatius' doctrine here is in full accord with the teaching of ascetical theology, that our fallen human nature requires not a few practices which are not strictly obligatory, hence of counsel, if we are to avoid mortal sin, and a *fortiori* venial offenses against God. According to Suarez, "It is impossible even for a lay person to be firmly resolved never to sin mortally unless he does some works of supererogation and has an explicit or at least virtual intention to perform them."[1]

[1] Francis Suarez, *De Religione*, Tract. IV, Lib. I, cap. 4, num. 12.

Assuming the first and second modes of humility to be already attained, if the will remains not merely indifferent to poverty or riches, honor or dishonor, but positively desires and chooses by preference poverty and dishonor in imitation of Christ, "this is the most perfect kind of humility." As explained by St. Ignatius in a little-known *Directory* written by himself, the fundamental difference between the second and third modes lies in the attitude of will towards poverty and humiliations, with all their implications. If the will is ready to accept them, but equally ready to embrace the opposite, we have the second mode; if it is not only willing to accept but actually prefers poverty and humiliations, we have the third. "If it is possible," Ignatius directs, "the exercitant should rise to the third grade of humility, in which, as far as he can, he is more inclined to what is more conformed to the evangelical counsels and the example of Christ our Lord, if the service of God be equal."[2] But if he inclines less to the counsels, as exemplified in the poverty and humiliation of Christ, at least he should be detached from riches and honors according to the second mode.

The author of the Exercises identifies the value of a retreat with a person's willingness to accept the evangelical counsels. He instructs the director professedly to "dispose the retreatant to desire the counsels rather than the precepts, if this be for the greater service of God." Consequently, "whoever has not reached the indifference of the second degree," which implies at least a passive acceptance of certain counsels, "should not be encouraged to make the election and will more profitably be given other exercises until he acquires this indifference."[3]

THEOLOGICAL PROBLEM

St. Ignatius twice uses the term "equal" to explain the service or glory given to God by the practice of humility. He de-

---

[2] *Monumenta Historica*, "Exercitia Spiritualia," p. 781.
[3] *Ibid.*, pp. 779, 781.

scribes the second mode as indifference to poverty, riches and the like, "provided only in either alternative I would promote equally the service of God our Lord and the salvation of my soul." In the third mode, I prefer poverty to riches, "supposing equal praise and glory to the Divine Majesty." However, the concept of "equal' is basically the same in both cases.

In the second mode, I evidently cannot remain indifferent to poverty or riches if I know that God would be better served and my salvation more assured by accepting riches instead of poverty. The moment I am faced with the prospect of any sin unless I choose one or the other, poverty or riches, honor or dishonor, I do not hesitate in choosing that which involves no offense against God. But given a situation where no sin (even venial) is involved, and in that sense as regards their essence my salvation and God's service are equally advanced through riches or poverty—I remain indifferent, i.e., equally disposed to accept poverty or riches, honor or dishonor. The condition, however, is always that God's service and my salvation would not be better promoted in a given instance if I preferred poverty to riches or vice versa.

The third mode of humility transcends mere indifference and actually prefers poverty and humiliation. This is an habitual disposition of will. Even so, I cannot prefer poverty, dishonor and contempt in any concrete circumstance if I know that God would be more glorified by the acceptance of riches and honor, as would be the case if the choice of poverty and humiliation involved sin or hindered the active apostolate. But "supposing equal praise and glory to the Divine Majesty," i.e., no question of sin or apostolic injury whether I prefer poverty or riches, honor or dishonor, then, in order "better to imitate Christ our Lord and be in reality more like Him, I desire and choose poverty with Christ poor, rather than riches; insults with Christ loaded with them, rather than honors; I desire to be accounted as worthless and a fool for Christ, rather than to be esteemed as wise and prudent in this world."

In the second and third modes, therefore, we have one element constant and the other variable. The constant is expressed by St. Ignatius' formula of "equal service of God," and means fidelity to the essential precepts of the Gospel and the good of souls. If this were absent, there would be unequal service of God, no matter how indifferent a person were to creatures or even preferred poverty and contempt to riches and honor. The variable factor is the attitude of will towards riches, honor, and their opposites. In the second mode, I am indifferent in this matter, and ready to accept poverty and humiliations (or enjoy riches and honor), and to that extent I have the spirit of the counsels, at least passively. But in the third mode, I am no longer indifferent; I prefer and desire the cross in imitation of Christ my Lord. Here is the full-flowering of Christian perfection, as St. Ignatius says, "where a person is more inclined to what is more conformed to the evangelical counsels and the example of Christ our Lord."[4]

The three modes can be illustrated by the example of a man who has unjustly suffered a grave injury to his honor:

First Mode: He does not care to retrieve his good name if it cannot be done without serious sin.

Second Mode: He will not try to defend his honor if this would involve committing venial sin; but if it can be done without sin, he wants to restore his reputation.

Third Mode: He considers the loss of reputation as profit in Christ. Instead of defending himself, he will gladly suffer the injury in silence. But on one condition: as long as God's glory is equally served, i.e., when neither a moral obligation nor benefit to others demands that he vindicate his legitimate rights. If such an obligation or benefit exists, then, *ipso facto* there is no longer equal glory to God, and he will defend his reputation without failing in the spirit of the third mode. All the while his internal dispositions are such that if a just defense of his honor were not obligatory in itself or profitable to the

4 *Ibid.,* p. 781.

neighbor, he will consider it a privilege to suffer in the company of his humiliated Master.[5]

RATIONALE OF THE THIRD MODE OF HUMILITY

The essence of the third mode of humility consists in preferring what is difficult, simply out of love for Christ, in order to be more like Him in poverty, humiliation and suffering. Unlike the first and second modes, the reasonableness of my attitude in the third degree is not so apparent, and except for the light of faith would be quite unintelligible.

Subjectively the motive for practicing the third degree is sheer love, expressed in the desire to be conformed to Christ, the Spouse of an ardent soul. No other reason is sought and none demanded. But objectively there is a deep reason why an earnest follower of Christ should wish to imitate Him in want and ignominy. It is the purpose of all pain and suffering, which is reparative and expiatory: reparation in restoring the honor which is owing to God's offended majesty, and expiation in removing the stain of guilt and debt of punishment which the sinner has incurred.

If I am looking for a reason to prefer poverty to riches and contempt to honor, I have it in my love for Christ. Love is by nature assimilable; it desires to be like the one loved. If I ask further why Christ, "for the joy set before Him chose the Cross," I find it in the mystery of Redemption. It was the will of His heavenly Father that the world should be redeemed not only by the Incarnation, but in the historical atmosphere of suffering and pain. In obedience to His Father, Christ chose to save the human race by enduring poverty, rejection, opposition and finally the disgrace of crucifixion although, absolutely speaking, the Redemption might have been accomplished by only a moment's pain. That Christ preferred this method of saving the world shows His wisdom in proving how much He loves us and how much we mean to Him; it also invites us to follow His example and prove our love for Him in return.

[5] *Opera Spiritualia Joannis P. Roothaan*, Vol. II, p. 117.

But the imitation of Christ in His suffering implies more than a way of proving our love for Him. It releases an energy which promotes the salvation of the world. The fact is a matter of faith; the explanation must be sought in the doctrine of the Mystical Body. For although the earthly life of Christ and His death more than sufficiently atoned for the sins of mankind, nevertheless by a "marvelous disposition of Divine Wisdom, we may complete those things that are wanting in the sufferings of Christ in our own flesh, for His body, which is the Church." This mystical identification of Christ with His members makes possible the application of His merits, gained by tribulation, to individual souls, beginning with our own and extending to all the human race, not only on earth but also in purgatory; and not only in the Church but also outside the Mystical Body. It was on this basis that Pius XI placed the effectiveness of reparation to the Sacred Heart. "In the degree to which our oblation and sacrifice more perfectly correspond to the sacrifice of Our Lord; that is, to the extent to which we have immolated love of self and our passions and crucified our flesh in that mystical crucifixion of which the Apostle writes, so much the more plentiful fruits of propitiation and expiation will we gain for ourselves and for others."[6]

The same idea was expressed from another viewpoint by Pius XII, in urging the imitation of Christ suffering for the benefit of the Mystical Body and the salvation of the modern world. Although His passion and death merited for the Church an infinite treasure of mercy, "God's inscrutable providence has decreed that these abundant graces should not be granted us all at once; and the amount of grace to be given depends in no small part also on our good deeds. They draw to the souls of men this ready flow of heavenly gifts granted by God. These heavenly gifts will surely flow more abundantly if we not only pray fervently to God . . . but if we also set our hearts on eternal treasures rather than the passing things of this world,

[6] Pius XI, Encyclical *Miserentissimus Redemptor*, in "Sacred Heart Encyclicals" (Carl Moell edit.), New York, pp. 38–40.

restrain this mortal body by voluntary mortification, denying it what is forbidden, forcing it to do what is hard and distasteful, and finally accept as from God's hands the burdens and sorrows of this present life." If there was never a time when the salvation of souls did not oblige us to associate our sufferings with those of the Redeemer, "that duty is clearer than ever today when a cosmic struggle has set almost the whole world on fire," and only Christ in His members can save it.[7]

In the meditation on the Kingdom it is imperative to have a correct notion of suffering and humiliation as instruments for personal sanctification antecedent to the apostolate. The more closely a man follows Christ, poor and contemned, the greater becomes his union with God and the more effective his labor for souls.

Another feature of the imitation of Christ, however, belongs to the apostolate itself. If we examine the pages of the Gospel, where do we find Christ practicing poverty, suffering humiliations and enduring contempt even to the death of the cross? Is it not in the very work of saving souls? Every action of Christ on earth was intrinsically apostolic in carrying out the mission of His Father to redeem the world. In imitating Him, we shall find that a large source of suffering in our lives stems from the apostolate. And the more zealous we are, the greater share of trials we shall have. St. Ignatius is warrant for the statement that "the greatest reward that a servant of God can receive for what he has done for his neighbor is scorn and contempt, the only reward that the world gave for the labors of its Divine Master."

St. Paul testified to how much a person must be ready to endure if he will follow Christ in the apostolate: ". . . in journeyings often, in perils in the city, in perils in the wilderness, in perils in the sea, in perils from false brethren; in labors and hardships, in many sleepless nights, in hunger and thirst, in fastings often, in cold and nakedness. Besides these outer

[7] Pius XII, Encyclical *Mystici Corporis Christi* (N.C.W.C. translation), 1943, pp. 66–67.

things, there is my daily pressing anxiety, the care of all the churches."[8] But in all of this, Paul was happy to suffer and gloried in the cross he was privileged to bear, because he saw himself not only imitating Christ to his own sanctification but cooperating with the Redeemer in the salvation of the world.

[8] II Corinthians 11:26–28.

7

The Retreat Election

A<small>LTHOUGH</small> the Election is not a special meditation, it is by all odds the most important single exercise of an Ignatian retreat. Whatever precedes, should prepare the exercitant to choose according to the highest motives; what follows will confirm the object of his choice. Some idea may be gained of the importance which St. Ignatius attached to the Election from the amount of space he devoted to its exposition: twenty pages of text in the *Monumenta Ignatiana*, or more than the Two Standards, Three Classes, and the Three Modes of Humility combined.

If there is one basic difference between the Spiritual Exercises and any other retreat method approved by the Church, it is the Election.

Fundamentally, the subject matter of the Election should be something good or indifferent in itself, and not opposed to the will of God. It may be the prospect of a new state of life, say, the priesthood, but not necessarily. It may be an improvement in the vocation that a person has already chosen, with a focus on that part of the spiritual life which needs special attention.

As will be apparent from the description which follows, the Election has universal applicability, ranging from an original decision to embrace a new mode of life, to improving one's conduct in a single area of a state already permanently undertaken. Correlative to the wide scope of subject matter are the kinds of people who can make the Election. In a sense, no one is excluded, although this requires explanation.

Strictly speaking, the object of an Election should be the evangelical counsels, undertaken, improved or reinvigorated, as the case may be. Since everyone, even lay persons, has been called to Christian perfection according to his state of life, the Ignatian Election pertains to anyone who has the grace of living out the counsels, whether in the world, in the priesthood, or under religious vows.

St. Ignatius prudently takes account of those who for some reason are incapable of making a regular Election, by providing them with "a method of amending and reforming their manner of life." Decisions made according to this method presume that a permanent vocation has already been embraced. The method itself primarily concerns people living in the world (whether laymen or priests) and stresses the right disposition of their external mode of life, in the use of temporal goods and the active apostolate. Particularly suited for those who make only a short retreat of two or three days, it cannot be given the full sweep of Christological motivation as conceived by the Exercises. Yet the scope of decision is practically unlimited: how to improve spiritually in one's profession or present employment, how to guide and direct those under authority, how to give an example of effective Christian living, how to apportion one's income between personal and family needs and the legitimate demands of charity.

The wide range of subjects on which the Election can be made has more than academic value. It neutralizes the suspicion, sometimes raised, about the usefulness of the Exercises for those who are already established in a fixed state of life or who are not bound by religious vows.

An excellent statement of the scope of the Election is given by Suarez, when treating of the function of the Spiritual Exercises:

Although one of the principal ends of the Spiritual Exercises is the election of a better state of life, they are by no means intended to have every retreatant choose the religious state. Unquestionably this way of life is more perfect in itself, but it may not be better for the one making the Election; and everyone should choose what is better for him. Not all people have the grace of this vocation and consequently should either choose another or at least adopt a mode of living that is more conducive to salvation. A religious, therefore, should no longer deliberate about a state of life; but he may well deliberate on how best to live in his vocation. Or, if that has been adequately considered, how to invigorate his motivation . . . how to become more diligent in overcoming obstacles and, in general, how to grow daily in performing actions that are most consistent with his religious profession. Lay people, too, even if they are going to remain in the world, have need of this help in order to obtain additional grace from God and prepare themselves to meet the dangers among which they live.[1]

Suarez, therefore, would have everyone make the Election, at least in a modified form, as St. Ignatius himself provides in a special method for reforming one's state of life.

TIME AND METHOD

St. Ignatius distinguishes three periods in a man's life, which may be repeated, when "a sound and good Election can be made." They are called "times" to describe the occasion when a person has certain internal experiences that are suitable for making an important decision in the presence of God. All three come within the ambit of the Exercises, but not all are equally practical or reliable for most exercitants.

FIRST TIME. When God our Lord so moves and attracts the will that a devout soul without hesitation, or the possibility of hesitation, follows what has been manifested to it. St. Paul and St. Matthew acted thus in following Christ our Lord.

In the nature of things, an Election rarely occurs under these circumstances. It represents a miraculous grace that should neither be asked for nor expected from God. When received,

[1] Francis Suarez, *De Religione*, Lib. IX, cap. 7, num. 15.

the will becomes almost passive and spontaneously responds to the efficacious action of the Holy Spirit.

SECOND TIME. When much light and understanding are derived through the experience of desolations and consolations, and discernment of diverse spirits.

This happens more frequently and, in fact, whenever inspirations and internal movements of the soul are so strong that, with a minimum of intellectual effort, the will is moved to a generous service of God. At times the consolation-experience (or its opposite) may practically equate the "first time." But normally the mind will have to exert itself to arrive at a moral decision, by distinguishing the positive sentiments of divine encouragement from the negative ones of human and diabolical despondency.

THIRD TIME. This is a time of tranquillity. First a man reflects why he was born, namely, to praise God and save his soul. With the desire to attain this end before his mind, he chooses as a means to the end a manner or state of life recognized by the Church that will help him in the service of God our Lord and the salvation of his soul.

In contrast with the preceding, this is the most ordinary and generally the most secure time for reaching a decision. Certainly it becomes highly effective when used to confirm the "second time," which depends on the discernment of spirits. Here the dominant attitude towards God is very active in using one's natural powers assisted by grace, before, during and after a decision has been reached. It also implies a certain trust in God's providence that needs to be stressed because, by supposition, I have less tangible evidence of the divine will in the absence of strong supernatural stimuli or of conflicting spiritual forces, as happens in the first and second "times."

Two extensive methods are provided for making the Election, and both refer to the "third time," when the soul peacefully reflects on its relations with God and "is not agitated by different spirits, but has the free and tranquil use of its natural powers." The value of these methods transcends their immediate function in the Exercises, since they can be used all through life—in modified, capsule form—to make any decision in the spiritual life, on any subject, and practically under any circumstances.

First Method: There are six steps in the first method, which follow in sequence from intellectual reflection, through prayer for light and strength, to a final decision offered to Almighty God.

The first step is "to place before my mind the object about which I want to make a choice." Characteristically, this initial requisite is to be supplied by the human exercitant, using the basic human faculty on which rests the whole supernatural life. The intellect isolates the area of decision.

The next step is also a mental operation: to focus my attention on the end for which I was created, along with an activity of will which is the fruit of all the preceding meditations. I put myself into a state of indifference, "like a balance at equilibrium," without leaning in favor of either side of the choice I am about to make.

At this stage, St. Ignatius requires a prayer of petition asking God "to deign to move my will and bring to my mind what I ought to do to promote His praise and glory." This is an essential condition because the matter in question is tied up with a supernatural end which cannot be attained without supernatural grace, and refers to the unknown future in which only God can direct my present decision in a way that will produce optimum results.

After prayer, I weigh the pros and cons, preferably written out in parallel columns, of the prospective Election. Spelling out the subject in this way has the advantage of reducing the whole problem to digestible size and allowing the mind to grasp all the main aspects in one intellectual glance. It also helps keep out extraneous factors which do not bear on the main issue and tend to obscure the judgment by appealing to the negative emotions of diffidence and fear.

Following this evaluation, the mind presents to the will what is obviously the most satisfactory choice to make. Then the classic Ignatian counsel: "I must come to a decision in the matter under deliberation because of weightier motives offered to my reason and not because of any sensual inclination." By insisting on the absolute necessity of coming to a decision, St. Ignatius cuts through the inveterate human tendency to procrastinate, especially in the larger issues of a man's life. And by laying down the rational norm for making a decision he eliminates the corresponding temptation to follow one's emotions, howsoever disguised, in choosing the best course of action on the road to salvation.

Finally another recourse to prayer, but only to offer a finished Election to God and ask Him to "confirm it if it is for His greater service and praise." The qualifying "if" is not a rhetorical flourish but shows the absence of any presumption that after all this scrutiny whatever I decide must be pleasing to the Divine Majesty. It is also an expression of confidence that providence is leading me to my appointed end, after I have done my part in finding the will of God.

Second Method: The alternate method of making an Election is somewhat shorter and approaches the problem from a different angle. It is more personal, psychological, and likely more appealing to many people. It is also more direct and dispenses with the minutiae of the first method, which makes it invaluable for settling those frequent, quick decisions that are part of our daily life.

Before deciding on a given question, first examine if your affection for a person, place, or course of action is dictated solely by the will of God. Do not proceed with a decision until this point is assured.

Place yourself in the position of another man with your choice to make. What advice would you give him? Give yourself the same.

Place yourself at the moment of death and consider what

decision you would then wish to have made. Make the same now.

Place yourself on Judgment Day and ask yourself what choice you would then wish to have made. Choose that course of action now.

After reaching a decision, offer the choice to God in prayer, asking Him to confirm it by His grace as in the previous method.

ELECTION COMPARED TO A CONVERSION

There is more than academic reason for comparing the Ignatian Election to a moral conversion. *Metanoia* or reformation of life runs as a theme through the pages of the Gospels; it is the object of Christ's exhortation in the Apocalypse of St. John; the Church's liturgy often exhorts us to turn away from creatures and be converted to God; and modern asceticism emphasizes the need of converting one's spiritual life by sublimating natural tendencies.

Comparing the Election with conversion does not imply that the two are coextensive. They are quite different in many ways, and yet their several points of contact should help to understand the Election in the more familiar terms of Scripture and Christian piety.

Implied Antecedents: The Election implies that a person's life is at least in some area not as perfectly dedicated to God as it might be; whereas a conversion suggests that the life is somehow or somewhat estranged from God.

Dominant Mode of Operation: While there are notable exceptions, at least the most common form of Election stresses the effort of the human mind and will, relying on the grace of God. In a conversion, however, the accent is on the operation of divine grace, which requires more or less cooperation on the part of the one converted.

Substantial Elements: The Election is essentially a decision to make a change for the better in one's relations with God. A conversion is the actual change in relation to God, which may

be: from disbelief to the fulness of the Catholic faith; from a
life of sin to friendship with God; from mediocrity to ordinary
piety; from ordinary piety to uncommon sanctity.

Time Factor: Election may involve a sudden decision to
change, certainly in the so-called "first time" of St. Ignatius.
But normally it comes only after long reflection and prayer. A
conversion, on the other hand, may be long-delayed and have
a backlog of dispositive circumstances, but the actual moral
change (as described by converts even among the saints) is a
rather sudden occurrence in the person's life.

Relation to Each Other: An Election may be considered an
inchoate conversion, from a less perfect to a more perfect service of God. A conversion, except in the case of a moral miracle,
is the result of at least an implicit decision to serve God more
faithfully.

Element of Change: In the Election, the object of the moral
change is something spiritually better in preference to what is
merely good. In a conversion, it is implied that the one being
converted is leaving what is somehow evil to embrace something that is good.

As found in the Scriptures and elsewhere, conversion has
only the generic concept of turning away from creatures and
coming back to God. But the Election of the Exercises is much
more refined. It supposes that a man is basically in God's
friendship and yet unduly attached to certain created things.
His decision, therefore, is to be *more* diverted from creatures
and to that extent *more* converted to God.

8

Contemplation for Obtaining Love

THE Contemplation for Obtaining Love is the masterpiece of the Spiritual Exercises. It offers an insight into Christian perfection at once so simple and yet profound as to escape the average retreatant unless he makes an effort to understand its theological implications.

Much as the Principle and Foundation anticipates in preview all the subsequent meditations, so the Contemplation epitomizes in retrospect and coordinates everything which precedes. But more significantly, where the Foundation describes the love of God for man in creating him for the Beatific Vision, the Contemplation should elicit a corresponding love for God in self-sanctification and labor for His greater glory.

Viewed in this light, the Contemplation becomes more than just another exercise of the retreat. Its function is to give a practical method for living out the "Contemplation in Action," which St. Ignatius so effectively promoted in his asceticism. By whatever name we call it: recollection, the presence of God, purity of intention, prayer in action, union with God —for Ignatius these were almost synonyms for something very specific. He identified them with the habitual practice of supernatural charity, not only during formal prayer or in the silence of the cloister, but in every action of daily life no matter how apparently trivial. What St. Paul urged upon the Corinthians, "Whether you eat or drink, or anything else you do, do all for the glory of God," Ignatius reduced to a simple form in his Contemplation for Obtaining Love.

71

He was not immediately concerned with evoking sentiments of affection for God. These he presumed to be present or at least not hard to arouse in a generous Christian soul. His main interest was to offer a plan of life for loving God in all creatures and them all in Him, not just occasionally but habitually, as a permanent disposition of heart. He wished to pass on to others what he had learned for himself, that "the only lawful ambition is to love God, and the price of this love is to love Him more," that "it is an extreme punishment to remain so long on earth, unless love causes us to live more in heaven and with God than on earth and with ourselves," that, finally, "he lives happily who, unceasingly, as far as he can, has his mind on God and God in his heart."[1] His plan was straightforward. He took the bare principle that love is active, and gave it universal application. "Do you want to love God in all things?" he asks the retreatant. "Then see the love of God manifest for you in every creature you touch, and you cannot help loving Him in return." The result is a spirit of recollection which transcends the attention to sensible and temporal affairs demanded by contact with the world and the work of the apostolate.

Since the Contemplation was meant to be practical, it may seem to have only a tenuous connection with speculative theology. Yet its foundations are rooted in dogmatic principles. We shall therefore first analyze the Church's teaching on the subjective love of God, that is, our love of God in response to His love for us, and then see where the present exercise fits into the concept of theological charity.

THEOLOGICAL ANALYSIS OF THE LOVE OF GOD

Charity as a theological virtue may be summarily described in terms of its relation to God, who may be loved egotistically or with perfect generosity. *Self-interested love of God* is also called the love of concupiscence, not because of any reference to the sense faculties but because God is loved for the benefits

---

[1] Xavier de Franciosi, *L'Esprit de Saint Ignace*, Paris, 1948, pp. 24–38.

we desire rather than for Himself alone. When this love looks to the future it can be equated with the virtue of hope, which may co-exist with supernatural charity but is really a distinct perfection of the will.

Disinterested or selfless love of God is technically the love of benevolence and so termed because it wills good to the one loved without looking for any advantage to self. In human relations, there may be true love of benevolence on one side only, where the love of one person meets no requital from the other. But in man's love of God this is impossible. Here the love is mutual since God always responds in kind to make our relationship the love of friendship, where the benevolence becomes effective in communicating from one to the other whatever can be freely exchanged.

The *motive* of supernatural charity (in the love of friendship) most clearly distinguishes it from all other virtues and, in practice, even from acts of charity which are not the perfect love of God. By way of parenthesis we may explain that the motive moves a faculty to action and determines its distinctive quality. Where, as in this case, the will is involved, the moving force must be goodness, whether real or apparent, created or divine. As defined by Catholic theology, the motive of supernatural charity is the absolute divine goodness, i.e., the goodness of God as it is in itself and not as beneficial to the person loving.

The divine goodness as an object of charity is nothing esoteric. It comprehends all the divine perfections: His infinite wisdom, power, liberality, mercy, magnanimity, beauty . . . whether taken together or (as most theologians teach) even taken singly.

These attributes may be considered under two aspects: *absolutely*, as they are in God, and *terminatively*, in so far as they produce some benefit in creatures. However, this does not mean that divine perfections like mercy and liberality cannot be the object of the love of benevolence, although certainly they bear a relation to the world outside of God. It all depends

on the aspect under which we consider them. Viewed as perfections proper to God, as emanating from Him, as deriving
from their source in His goodness, they are adequate motives
for making an act of perfect love of God. But taken from the
creature's viewpoint as benefits to me, either individually or
as a member of society, God's liberality and mercy are the objects of hope or gratitude, but not formally of theological
charity. Charity may indeed arise from hope and gratitude,
and these may be present along with charity, but the latter is
itself motivated by no personal benefit accrued or desired. Its
motive is the divine perfections *in so far as they are God's*.
Some theologians deliberately avoid using the term "relative"
as distinct from "absolute" divine attributes, in order not to
leave the wrong impression that such realities in God as mercy
and magnanimity (though evidently related to creatures) are
outside the scope of perfect charity. The adverbs *terminatively*
and *respectively* are preferred, to describe the divine perfections when viewed from their *terminus ad quem*, or the creatures who are benefited. Under this aspect, they fall short of
being proper objects of the love of benevolence, since they are
rather motives for the love of concupiscence which looks to
self-advantage.

The material object of disinterested charity, though pri-
marily God Himself, also includes the person loving as well as
his neighbor. Indeed, everything which increases the divine
glory is indirectly related to the secondary object of charity.
This follows logically from the perfect love of God. If I love
Him, I must love what He loves, and for the same reason.
Among the objects of His love are myself and my neighbor.
He loves us with complete selflessness, out of sheer liberality.
Therefore within the ambit of theological charity are included,
besides God, all the objects of His beneficent will—notably
myself and my fellowman. Yet the motive even in loving myself is not self-interest but God, here seen in the exercise of
liberality towards me.

A problem inherent in this question may be solved by the

distinction between objective fact and psychological motivation. Objectively, no doubt, by loving God I benefit myself;
since inevitably my love for Him tends to an ultimate union
with God and eternal beatitude. But psychologically or subjectively the motive that moves my will to love God with perfect benevolence is not self-perfection. It is the goodness of
God for itself, not for the profit which I derive.

Our love for God is naturally demonstrative, since genuine
charity cannot remain sterile and our benevolence towards the
Creator will not be unproductive. It manifests itself internally
by acts of affection and externally by effective deeds.

Internal acts of affection are called "internal" with reference to the will, and comprehend all the elicited acts of volition, which begin and terminate in the will faculty. Thus *joy
and complacency* are stimulated by reflecting on the perfections of God: His holiness and beauty, His infinite wisdom and
power, His boundless mercy and liberality. According to St.
Francis de Sales, "when we have brought our understanding
to consider the greatness of the goods that are in this Divine
object, it is impossible that our wills should not be touched
with complacency in this good. Then we use the liberty we
have to provoke our heart to redouble and strengthen its first
complacency by acts of approbation and rejoicing."[2] In a
word, we are pleased to see the greatness of God and, without
envy, join with Him in rejoicing over His perfections.

Along with complacency arises the *desire to increase the
divine goodness* as far as possible, since benevolence means
just that; except that God is infinite and cannot be enriched
by anything we do. If there is question of God's intrinsic perfections, then, except by a fiction of the mind, we cannot desire to increase them.

But there is no imagination or hypothesis when it comes to
desiring an increase in God's external glory, which consists in
the knowledge and love that created souls have for Him on

[2] St. Francis de Sales, *Treatise on the Love of God*, Westminster, Md.,
1942, p. 196.

earth, in purgatory, and in the Beatific Vision. And here we come to grips with the important problem of whether and how it is possible to desire union with God in heaven as an object of perfect charity. The most authentic answer to this question has been given by St. Alphonsus Liguori, and needs to be quoted verbatim:

Dubium: Is the desire to enjoy God the object of charity?

Response: Yes, it is. For charity tends to God as the final end, and therefore to desire to enjoy Him who is our final end is not only a proper act of charity, it is the most perfect because fruition is consummate charity. That is why the Apostle's desire to die and to be with Jesus Christ was a perfect act of charity. St. Augustine expressly says the same thing: 'I call charity the movement of the soul tending towards the enjoyment of God for His own sake.' Neither does this make the object of charity the same as the object of hope, which also seeks to enjoy God. For while charity tends to the same enjoyment for the glory of God Himself, hope reaches for the possession of God as an advantage to us. Moreover, when a man is enjoying God he becomes oblivious of himself and loves Him with all his powers. Consequently, if a man looks upon the divine benefits as a communication of the goodness of God, he places a real act of charity, because what he loves in these benefits is not the advantage of the creature who receives them, but the goodness of God who dispenses them.[3]

Finally, among the internal acts of supernatural charity, *sorrow for sin* follows spontaneously on the desire to see God duly honored and loved. When I reflect on my own sins and those of others, I am grieved at the injury done to the Divine Majesty and wish to make amends for the offenses committed against God.

External acts of the love of God are the effective counterparts of internal affection. They are called "external" in relation to the will and include every type of activity, of whatever faculty, that may be commanded or directed by the power of volition. As conceived by Christian asceticism, they are an

[3] St. Alphonsus Liguori, *Homo Apostolicus*, Regensburg, 1862, Vol. I, tract. 4, cap. 1, pp. 117–118.

essential part of any genuine love of friendship, which consists precisely in the exchange of any goods that are separately possessed. Fundamentally these acts are of two kinds: those involving labor for the glory of God and those concerned with reparation for sin. On the first level, the desire to advance God's glory is manifested (beyond mere affection) by using every means at our disposal to *grow in personal sanctity*, and doing everything in our power to increase the knowledge and love of God in the souls of others through the *apostolate*. And obversely, the sorrow we feel over sin urges us to the practice of *penance and mortification* to expiate these crimes and offer satisfaction to the Divine Majesty.

Following St. Thomas, theologians require four conditions to acquire the perfect love of God:

Recollection of God's benefits, since all that we have, in body and soul and external possessions, has come from Him. Consequently to love Him with a perfect heart, we must earnestly reflect on everything He has given to us.

Meditation on the divine perfections. For God is greater than our heart; and though we study Him with all our heart and strength, yet we do not exhaust His greatness.

Detachment from things of this world, since the heart of man is too small where God is concerned. If you take in creatures, you drive out God.

Avoidance of all sin. For no one can love God while living in [mortal] sin, as Christ tells us, "You cannot serve God and mammon." If you are in sin, you do not love God.[4]

There is a difference, however, between the first and second pair of conditions given by St. Thomas. The first two are normal psychological requisites for obtaining and increasing divine love; the last two are essential qualities without which charity does not exist. In order to make an act of the perfect love of God, I must love Him above all things, i.e., I must be ready to lose everything, even life itself, rather than offend

---

[4] St. Thomas, *De Duobus Praeceptis Caritatis* (Opuscula Omnia), Paris, 1927, Vol. IV, p. 420.

Him by mortal sin—which corresponds to the first mode of humility in the Spiritual Exercises.

ASCETICAL APPLICATION

Against the background of the preceding analysis of super-natural charity we are in a better position to evaluate the *Contemplatio ad Amorem*. Since the latter is essentially practical and intended to serve as an ascetical method of growing in the love of God, we should not expect St. Ignatius to touch on every phase of charity as outlined in manuals of theology; although he makes a remarkably full coverage of the subject, even in the few paragraphs of the Contemplation. What he does, however, and what can be very useful to know in directing (or making) the Exercises is the aspects which he emphasizes and the coloring he gives to certain features. In this way, the principles of divine love are reduced to an easy and more effective practice.

Two Principles of Love: The two principles which St. Ignatius sets down at the beginning of the exercise summarize the accent he wants to place in cultivating the love of God. First is an insistence on effective charity as distinct from the merely affective. "Love," he says, "should manifest itself in deeds rather than in words." A number of reasons suggest themselves for making such a distinction.

Since the love of God finds its best analogy on earth in human relations, say, in the love of husband and wife, it is imperative to see the latter in its substance and cleared of accidentals. Among these the most liable to be taken for true love are emotionalism and sentimentality, expressed in beautiful words and melody, but lacking the generosity of true sacrifice.

History is filled with examples of men and women who professed to love God, but their actions belied their words. Ignatius recognized that the human will can deceive itself into believing it loves God because it repeats a verbal formula, the while indulging in certain practices that are incompatible with true affection. "If you love Me," Christ said, "keep My commandments" (John 14:15).

St. Ignatius does not deny that love consists also in words. But actions speak louder than words. In fact, they are words, thundering declarations which prove more eloquently than speech where a man's affections really lie.

The basic principle of asceticism involved here is the relative emphasis on grace and free will. To love God in word may be perfectly sincere. "No one can say, 'Lord Jesus,' except by the Holy Spirit" (I Cor. 12:3). There may be no question of masking a false interior behind affectionate sentiments. It does make a difference, however, where we concentrate our efforts. It is not at all impossible, as Reformation theology proved, to stress faith and love so much that good works are overlooked or even despised. But we are not mere pawns in the almighty hands of God. We have to work out our salvation: with divine grace, of course, but work it out no less. And if we ask where human effort is more required: in verbal statements or in actual deeds, the answer is rhetorical.

St. Ignatius' second principle stresses the mutuality and communication in true love of friendship, which consists in sharing what each one possesses. This clarifies the difference between love of concupiscence and the love of benevolence. "Love of concupiscence," says Francis de Sales, "is founded on a hope of deriving some benefit from the object of our affection; love of benevolence produces affection for a person with no reference to our interests. To have a love of benevolence for anyone means to wish him well, to desire him every blessing and happiness."[5] Therefore even our love for God, who has everything, must be disinterested to be perfect; must seek rather to please Him than satisfy ourselves, although objectively we derive the highest self-satisfaction in giving ourselves to God.

A further clarification of St. Francis de Sales explains the two kinds of benevolence we may have towards a person:

[5] *Treatise on the Love of God*, p. 51.

If the one to whom we wish good already possesses it, then we wish it to him by the pleasure and contentment we have to see him possessed of it, and hence springs the love of complacency, which is simply an act of the will by which it is joined and united to the pleasure, content and good of another. But in case the person to whom we wish good has not yet obtained it, we desire him to have it and consequently that love is termed the love of desire.

Both are verified in our love of God. We have the love of complacency as regards His intrinsic perfections, and the love of desire as regards His external glory.

Purpose of the Contemplation: According to St. Ignatius, the purpose of the Contemplation is fourfold, where each preceding end becomes a means to the further end that follows. The exercitant should ask "for an intimate *knowledge* of the many blessings received, that filled with *gratitude* for everything, I may in all things *love* and *serve* the Divine Majesty." First is knowledge of God's benefits, which leads to gratitude, inducing love that terminates in the service of God.

This sequence corresponds exactly with St. Thomas' first two requisites for obtaining charity. The last two, detachment from creatures and avoidance of sin, are amply treated by St. Ignatius in the Principle and Foundation, the Three Classes and the Modes of Humility. Moreover St. Thomas, in common with Christian tradition, holds that reflection on divine blessings is a *necessary* condition for arriving at the perfect love of God. In fact, he makes this reflection the first condition required. Consequently, in the ordinary disposition of providence, unless there is a previous consideration of God's goodness in my regard, I will not rise to the perfect love of true friendship.

I am instinctively grateful to God once I realize how good He has been to me. But the next step, from gratitude to love, is the most crucial in the whole Contemplation. The question is how gratitude to God for His benefits becomes an act of disinterested charity. Or put differently: in what sense is the

⁶ *Ibid.*

love of gratitude a pre-condition for the love of benevolence? Suarez gives the answer by distinguishing an imperfect and perfect love of gratitude. In imperfect love, we are grateful to God for the profit accrued to us. However:

> When God is loved perfectly for His benefits, He is rather loved because He loves us. This is true charity and friendship, since the objective reason for the act is not outside the divine goodness. For the love by which God loves us is God Himself, and one of His highest perfections. Furthermore, He loves us because He is good; so that when we love Him for loving us, we love Him because of His goodness.[7]

We may add that psychologically it is quite impossible to reflect on God's blessings without becoming conscious of His goodness, from which the benefits proceed. Spontaneously, under the influence of grace, the will is drawn to complacency at the source of this bounty and places an act of perfect love.

The final stage from love to service is the familiar Ignatian stress on effective charity which goes beyond internal sentiment. Also any obscurities about the nature of service on which St. Ignatius insists throughout the Exercises, from the Principle and Foundation on, are clarified in the present context, where the service of God becomes the highest degree of theological charity, animated by the purest love of God.

Four Aspects of God's Benefits: St. Ignatius has the exercitant review God's benevolence towards man under four aspects, each offering a new insight into the divine goodness and calling forth a corresponding love in me.

At the broadest level, I am told to "recall to mind the blessings of creation and redemption, and the special favors I have received." Significantly, God does not love me with mere affection *ad intra* (within Himself) but effectuates His love *ad extra* (outside Himself), by bringing me out of nothing into existence, raising me to a supernatural destiny, restoring me after I had fallen, and in a thousand ways showering me with His gifts and graces. On my part, this should evoke a *respon-*

[7] Francis Suarez, *De Caritate*, Disp. I, Sect. 2, num. 3.

sive desire to give all that I can to God and not remain satisfied with interior sentiments of love. Hence the *Suscipe* is my answer to the *Suscipe* of God. He has exhausted His generosity to me, so I want to exhaust mine towards Him, praying:

Take, O Lord, and receive all my liberty, my memory, my understanding, and all my will, all that I have and possess. Thou hast given all these to me; to Thee I restore them. All are Thine, dispose of them all according to Thy will. Give me Thy love and Thy grace, for this is enough for me.

The second reflection rises to a higher plane, recalling how God not only gives me so many gifts, including myself, but literally dwells in the creatures He donates, "in the elements giving them existence, in the plants giving them life, in the animals conferring on them sensation, in man bestowing understanding. So He dwells in me and gives me being, life, sensation, intelligence, and makes a temple of me." Again a corresponding desire should be educed in me, not only to give to God all that I have and do, but as far as possible to give myself along with my gifts. There is such a thing as "putting my heart into what I am doing," intensifying the generosity and fervor of my donation, and so equating in analogous fashion the presence of God in His blessings to me.

But God does more than communicate His presents, and more than dwell in them. I should further consider "how God works and labors for me in all creatures upon the face of the earth." As far as it can be said, God "exerts" Himself in giving me the blessings of nature and grace, which He proved conclusively in becoming man for my salvation; and laboring, suffering and dying to show His love for me. Once more, this should produce a *similar* response in me. In the spirit of the third mode of humility—which now becomes the third mode of love—I should not only be generous towards God in working for His glory, and not only put myself whole-heartedly into what I am doing, but I should work "as one who is laboring," with real exertion and effort and, if need be, at the cost of suffering and pain.

Finally, at the highest level, St. Ignatius tells me to "consider all blessings and gifts as descending from above. Thus, my limited power comes from the supreme and infinite power above, and so, too, my justice, goodness and mercy, descend from above as rays of light descend from the sun, or as the waters flow from their fountains." What, we ask, is the real purpose that God has in giving me so many gifts, in which He dwells and continues to labor? To give me Himself. His benefits are all creatures, and intended to lead me to possess the Creator. If I am in His friendship, this possession on earth is enjoyed as "through a mirror in an obscure manner," but in heaven "face to face." As the rays of light descending from the sun unite the sun and earth by means of their common light, and as waters flowing from their fountains join the remotest tributary with its primal source, so in the order of grace by means of His gifts God wishes to join Himself to me. The mystery is that even here I am free to make a voluntary response in kind, giving to God what I have, with generosity and sacrifice, while intending these gifts as projections of myself towards an eternal union with God.

Contemplation in Action: The Contemplation offers a clear synthesis of St. Ignatius' most distinctive contribution to the science of asceticism. Having in mind people like himself, who were living the mixed life of prayer and the external apostolate, he proposed as the guiding star of Christian perfection "to see God in all creatures, and them all in Him." In this way, the apostle or the man in the world, in spite of a welter of activity, can remain in contact with God. The secret is to put into practice the Contemplation not only as an isolated and formal prayer but as a constant attitude of mind and disposition of heart.

Inevitably the man of action, priest, religious or layman, will have creatures impinge on his consciousness every moment of the day. The way in which he uses them will determine how much of an active contemplative he becomes. If he has trained himself to look upon creatures as vehicles of the

Creator, in which He dwells and labors, and through which He communicates His gifts and Himself, creatures will cease to be obstacles and become instead the very means by which the soul remains united with God.

Ignatius assumes, however, that I have learned two simple but very profound truths: that nothing happens by chance with God because He wills or permits every creature that enters my daily life, no matter how transient; and that God's purpose in sending these creatures is precisely to evoke a realization of His activity in my favor and a corresponding reaction on my part "in favor of" God. When making the Contemplation in retreat time, I try to have this conviction sink deep into my deposit of faith—that creatures and Creator are related as means to end, being used by God to manifest His love for me and intended by Him to stimulate my love for God.

II

Ignatian Ideals and Methodology

9

On Examining One's Conscience

A CURSORY reading of what St. Ignatius says about examination of conscience reveals a number of simple facts. He recommends two kinds of examen, a general and particular. Where the general examen covers all our defects, the particular concentrates on one fault or sin for a definite length of time. Among the areas to be examined generally, special attention should be paid to our speech, notably idle words and failings against charity. The particular examination is made twice a day and recalled briefly on rising in the morning; by keeping a written account of the number of faults per half day, we can see our improvement (or otherwise) from day to day and take proper measures accordingly.

Behind this plain façade of methodology lies a wealth of ascetical principles and psychological insight that goes back to the early centuries of the Church. By the daily search into our every action, wrote Chrysostom, we shall make easy and rapid progress towards the highest perfection.

Modern psychology emphasizes the need of specifying the will act for maximum volitional activity. As a general rule, the more definite and circumscribed a prospective course of action, the more effectively will it be put into execution. The lag and discrepancy between resolution and achievement are common experience. How to make the real more closely approach the ideal? Superficially it would seem the more earnest our resolutions the better results we can expect. Yet, without minimizing the importance of energetic beginnings, the main factor is sustained motivation, whether I resolve on a series of actions like the practice of charitable speech, or a single act like the acceptance of a grave humiliation. In either case what I need at the time the performance is due are clear motives in the shape of strong convictions that this should be done and this is the way to do it. Here the examination of conscience becomes indispensable. If I have resolutely decided on avoiding sharp criticism whenever I am crossed, this judgment becomes a thought pattern in my life, which I reenforce every time I make an internal review. Comes an occasion that provokes my patience and immediately I recall the decision to control myself and keep my tongue—supported by all the motives that I have placed behind the resolution.

However, the previous examination of future acts does more than guarantee motivation for the will. It also supplies systematization for the mind. If I have carefully thought through a specific action I want to perform, when the time comes for effecting it, I know what I am supposed to do. Being charitable to a difficult person may involve more than biting my tongue. It may require diplomacy to avoid needless exposure to irritating situations; it may call for speaking kindly to the very man who would normally provoke me; it will always require some adaptation to circumstances which I can wisely anticipate and master because of my anticipation.

This can be highly effective in overcoming unwelcome thoughts. By regularly recalling the kind of thoughts I wish to control and planning on a positive method of controlling them, I give myself the best assurance of success. The reason is that thoughts are more elusive than overt actions; the power of the will over them is described by Aristotle as diplomatic instead of despotic. I cannot say to my mind, "Don't think of this," as I would to my hand, "Don't touch that," and hope for immediate response. I need to substitute another thought-complex for the undesirable one and hope that the latter will be driven into the subconscious. Through the examination of conscience I foresee what actions can be substituted for the usual ones, with consequently different thoughts evoked in the mind. I may have found that certain reading—perhaps innocuous in itself—brings on a train of thought that will cause me trouble with carnal images or difficulties about the faith. The foresight gained by examination will recommend changes in my reading habits, with corresponding freedom from disturbance in the mind. I can even use my examination to plan on what kind of thoughts to substitute for the bad ones; how I should maintain myself in peace when the disturbances arise; and how to divert my attention to what is attractive, but harmless, and away from what is attractive but potentially sinful.

Theology aside, even natural psychology teaches the wisdom of prudent foresight and internal scrutiny. Arnold Bennett, who was no theologian, forty years ago wrote a little work on the science of self-direction, in which he recommended periodic examination before the bar of reason. "Happiness," he said, "does not spring from physical or mental pleasure, but from the development of reason and the adjustment of conduct to principles. A life in which conduct does not fairly well accord with principles is a silly life; and that conduct can be made to accord with principles only by means of daily examination, reflection and resolution."[1]

The classic example of a man far removed from the cloister and even from orthodox Christianity who used the examination to good effect is Benjamin Franklin. "I made a little book," he says in his Autobiography,

in which I allotted a page for each of the virtues. I rul'd each page with red ink, so as to have seven columns, one for each day of the week, marking each column with a letter for the day. I cross'd these columns with thirteen red lines, marking the beginning of each line with the first letter of one of the virtues, on which line, and in its proper column, I might mark, by a little black spot, every

---

[1] Arnold Bennett, *How to Live on Twenty-Four Hours a Day,* New York, 1910, pp. 71–72.

fault I found upon examination to have been committed respecting that virtue upon that day.[2]

Franklin gave a week's attention to each of thirteen virtues successively, beginning with temperance and ending with humility. "Proceeding thus, I could go through a course compleat in thirteen weeks, and four courses in a year." It is not clear where he got the idea, perhaps from the student guide books in Jesuit-conducted schools in France. But whatever the source, he attributed most of his success in life to this practice of acquiring "the habitude of all the virtues."

SPIRITUAL CONFESSION

The practice of spiritual communion is well established among the faithful and needs no apology or promotion here. It means an ardent desire of the soul to be united with Christ in the Eucharist and, therefore, a communion in spirit which looks forward to sacramental communion in reality.

Comparable to spiritual communion is the examination of conscience as a spiritual reception of the sacrament of penance.

In the sacrament of confession, the penitent must relate his sins to the priest; in a private examination of conscience the confession is made directly to God. In the sacrament there must be sorrow for the sins confessed, at least attrition through fear of divine justice, otherwise the absolution takes no effect; in the examen the same is true, except that mortal sins are not forgiven without perfect contrition motivated by the love of God. For both the sacrament and examination one test of a sincere contrition is the firm purpose of amendment. The absolution in the sacrament is given by a priest in the name of the truine God; in private examens the Holy Trinity effects the remission by direct operation on the human soul. Finally, to complete the analogy, satisfaction for sins confessed sacramentally is essentially covered by the penance imposed by the

[2] *Memoirs of the Life and Writings of Benjamin Franklin*, New York, 1927, p. 101.

priest; in the examination, the penance is self-imposed, yet not without the guiding impulse of the Holy Spirit.

But the relation between the sacrament of confession and daily examination goes beyond even this close comparison. The two are mutually dependent. Theologians commonly teach that the sacraments give unequal graces to different persons, depending on their varying dispositions of soul. What the Council of Trent says concerning baptism, that it confers grace "according to each person's own disposition and cooperation," applies to the other sacraments, including confession. Therefore, the better we are prepared spiritually when approaching the tribunal of penance, the more and greater graces we may expect from the sacrament thus received. In other words, the more humility and charity we have, the greater our detachment from creatures and attachment to the will of God, the more of sacramental blessings we shall be given. The genius of the daily examen consists in its ability to produce these valuable dispositions antecedent to sacramental confession. What better means to induce humility or charity than a courageous look at our sins and gratitude to God for His mercies? What surer way of becoming freed from unruly affections and firmly rooted in God than reflection on how creatures have betrayed us and how the Creator only cannot be loved too much?

If examination of conscience disposes the soul for greater graces in the sacrament of penance, it also implements these graces and carries them into consequent effect. Certainly the purpose of confession is not only the remission of sins, but also the improvement of morals and growth in the spiritual life— for which the daily examination becomes a valuable aid.

Experience and faith tell us we need God's grace and a determined will to overcome the sins and defects we regularly confess. The degree of our determination can be safely gauged by the willingness to submit our habitual failings to an objective daily scrutiny, comparing one day's progress or failure with the next and taking practical measures to avoid the occasions

of our moral defects. The more firm our purpose of amendment, the more seriously we should undertake this methodical
self-examination. On the side of divine grace, we know that
the ordinary means of obtaining God's help is confident and
assiduous prayer; and not just prayer *in globo,* but specific petitions requesting specific needs. Daily examination furnishes
the framework for this kind of prayer. I have been failing in
patience whenever confronted with a situation. As I examine
my failure yesterday, I anticipate a recurrence and pray for
light and strength to cope with the same problem tomorrow.
When tomorrow comes and the provocation arises, I am fore-
armed with grace merited by yesterday's prayer and the result
is a moral victory instead of another defeat.

TWO KINDS OF EXAMEN

The two examens, general and particular, differ more widely
than seems implied in their respective names. In the text of
the Exercises, the particular examen comes first, not only in
sequence but in objective importance. St. Ignatius called it
the "particular and *daily* examen," to be distinguished from
the general examen whose purpose is to purify the soul and
better prepare it for sacramental confession. This does not
mean that the particular examen only is made every day, but
that part of its essential character is to go over a specified
moral deficiency with daily, uninterrupted regularity.

While St. Ignatius did not invent the particular examen, he
reduced it to methodical form and made it so intrinsic to
the Spiritual Exercises that as the retreat movement spread
throughout the world, the particular examen became the stock-
in-trade of modern asceticism. Already in ancient times the
pagan philosopher, Pythagoras, obliged his disciples to examine
themselves twice daily, morning and evening, on three questions: What have I done? How have I done it? What have I
failed to do? And among the Christian Fathers, St. Basil promised the early monks that, "You will certainly grow in virtue

if you make a daily account of your actions and compare them with the previous day."[3]

The wisdom of the particular examen lies deeper than the old maxim, *"Divide et impera."* Evidently we have a better chance to master our tendencies if we take them one at a time and concentrate our efforts on pride, lust, or laziness, instead of scattering volitional energy over the whole field of our passions. But among the aberrations some are more prominent than others, and among these one generally predominates. If I can isolate these dominant tendencies, manifested in a certain pattern of my sins, and work on them, my labor will not only be more effective because less dissipated, but will be directed at the source of my evil inclinations. I shall be laying the axe to the root of the tree. St. Francis de Sales as a young man was given to melancholy which sometimes bordered on despair. He specialized in overcoming despondency to the point where he became the modern apostle of a joyous confidence in God. Matt Talbot had to fight an irrational thirst for drink, which he conquered through concentrated prayer and reached high sanctity in the process. From the standpoint of providence, God permits us to have master passions or weaknesses because He intends them as instruments of our sanctification. They serve to deflate our self-sufficiency and constrain us, as nothing else, to betake ourselves to God in humble and constant prayer which is the touchstone of sanctity.

The general examen has a wider scope than the particular. Its object is to keep the soul alert on all that pertains to the service of God. Here also St. Ignatius was no innovator. But his succinct method for making the general examen has become standard in ascetical literature.

Before examining my sins, I first thank God for the favors bestowed on me in the past and ask Him for light to know my failings and strength to overcome them. The examination itself should be systematic, following in sequence the hours of the day and passing over my thoughts, words and actions in

[3] St. Basil, "Sermo de Renuntiatione Saeculi," PL 3, 647.

that order. Then I ask God to have mercy on me and promise, with His help, to avoid these offenses in the future.

One aspect of the general examen that may be overlooked is its function of cleansing the soul of moral guilt. Its highpoint is clearly the sorrow we excite over our sins, while begging forgiveness for having offended God. Hence the need of recognizing on doctrinal grounds that both guilt and punishment may be remitted outside the sacrament of penance, including mortal sins, if these are repented with perfect sorrow which includes the intention of later confessing to a priest. Some theologians believe that imperfect contrition will remit venial sins without sacramental absolution; they are certainly forgiven if the sorrow is perfect. When the Council of Trent defined contrition as "a deep sorrow and detestation for sin committed, with the resolution of sinning no more," it was stating a general principle that applies to contrition outside and within the confessional. Through the daily examination of conscience, therefore, a person can literally purify his soul of the stains contracted by sin and thus become daily more fit to receive in greater abundance the blessings that God reserves for the pure of heart.

As commonly understood, the term "examination of conscience" looks only to the correction and forgiveness of sins and moral failings. But St. Ignatius did not make the practice so exclusive. In the First Method of Prayer he provides for self-examination on the seven capital sins not only negatively but also positively—and that in two ways. He recommends that "the contrary virtues be considered," e.g. purity, "in order to understand better the faults committed that come under the seven capital sins." Moreover, and still more positively, "in order the better to avoid these sins, one should resolve to endeavor by devout exercises to acquire and retain the seven virtues contrary to them." According to the Spanish editors of the Spiritual Exercises, a distinction should be made between the use of the examens during and outside of retreat time. When actually making the retreat, the particular examen is intended primarily to remove whatever faults are committed in the process of going through the Exercises; whereas outside of retreat, this examination should be used not only for extirpating sins and imperfections but also for positively cultivating particular virtues. The general examen, on the other hand, acts as a corrective for sins and evil tendencies at all times, whether during a retreat or otherwise.[4]

VALUE OF THE EXAMENS

It may come as a surprise that the daily examination of conscience is so highly regarded by the Church as an instrument of sanctification for all classes of people in every station of life.

Priests and clerics in general are urged by Canon Law to make a daily examination of conscience, which Pius XII called "the most efficacious means we have for taking account of our spiritual life during the day, for removing the obstacles which hinder our spiritual life or retard one's progress in virtue, and for determining on the most suitable means to assure to our ministry greater fruitfulness and to implore from the heavenly Father indulgence upon so many of our deeds wretchedly done."[5]

Religious institutes of men and women universally provide an appointed time each day for examination of conscience. Some of the most practical directions left by the founders elaborated on the merits of this practice. St. Vincent de Paul, who was schooled in the Spiritual Exercises, instructed the Daughters of Charity to make a particular examen on their predominant faults not only twice daily at the usual time, but frequently during the day they should ask themselves, "What did I resolve to do?" If it was to mortify impatience, let them reflect, "How have I acted?" And if they have acted patiently under irritation, "Thank God"; if not "then beg for forgiveness and impose a penance on yourself. For it is impossible to

---

[4] Monumenta Historica, "Exercitia Spiritualia," pp. 12–13.
[5] Pius XII, Apostolic Exhortation Menti Nostrae, N.C.W.C. Translation, 1951, pp. 19–20.

correct a bad habit without perfect fidelity in this matter."[6]
St. Ignatius valued the examens so highly that in his own life-
time the twice-daily examination was the only mental prayer
he prescribed for his young religious. The other half hour of
prayer was optionally vocal or mental and more easily dis-
pensed from, but the examens were indispensable.

Less familiar is the practice of daily examination of conscience among the laity as a fruit of the Spiritual Exercises. A
recent study of the prayer habits of Catholic lay leaders showed
a close relation between their use of the examen and the annual retreat. After a closed retreat of more than three days, the
ratio of fidelity to the daily examination was over seventy per
cent. At the other extreme, the custom was rare among those
who had never gone through the Spiritual Exercises. If we
recall that from the beginning St. Ignatius gave the Exercises
to people whose vocation was to remain in the world, and that
self-examination is co-essential with prayer as the foundation
of Christian perfection, the only wonder is that more lay persons have not been encouraged to undertake the practice.

When Francis de Sales wrote the *Introduction to a Devout
Life* for people in the world, he prescribed an examination of
conscience every evening and urged his readers "never to omit
this exercise," suggesting the Ignatian sequence which begins
with "thanking God for preserving you during the day," and
end with "a resolution to make an early confession and diligently to amend if you have sinned in thought, word, or
deed."[7] This recommendation was the outgrowth of the author's own formation in the Exercises of St. Ignatius, from his
boyhood as a sodalist in the Jesuit college in Paris to his annual
retreat of ten days as priest and bishop of Geneva. The Spiritual Exercises, he used to say, have made as many saints as they
contain letters; and intrinsic to the Exercises are the daily ex-
aminations.

[6] *Conferences of St. Vincent de Paul*, Vol. IV, Westminster, Maryland,
1952, p. 214.
[7] St. Francis de Sales, *Introduction to a Devout Life*, New York, 1923, p. 73.

A word of explanation may be added on the Sulpician method of making the examination of conscience. Popularized by Cardinal de Bérulle, Olier and others, it retains intact the principle of the Ignatian examens, but adds some modifications. Its purpose is not directly (albeit ultimately) to correct moral failings or acquire specific virtues, but rather to cleanse ourselves of those evil dispositions which impede the action of Christ on the soul and resist the inspirations of His grace. Consequently the basic idea of the Sulpician method is to foster union with the Incarnate Word by internal acts of adoration and love, and striving to imitate the virtues of the Son of God. On closer analysis this method appears to be an extension of the Ignatian examen and includes other forms of prayer like the meditations and contemplations of the Spiritual Exercises.

10

Vocal and Mental Prayer

IT WOULD be a mistake to suppose that the theory and practice of prayer found in the Spiritual Exercises refer only to the time of retreat. They have universal application and contain the refined wisdom of one of the Church's greatest mystics on the subject of the soul's communication with God, from the lowliest type of vocal prayer to the highest form of contemplation.

Some of the rules and directives like the "Remote and Proximate Preparation" are useful for any kind of prayer at any time. Others like the familiar triad of prelude, points and colloquy are more pertinent to meditation. Still others, described in the Exercises as "The Three Methods of Prayer," are a supplement to ordinary meditation and though primarily intended to help beginners in the spiritual life, they can be profitably used by anyone else.

PREPARATION FOR PRAYER

Since formal prayer is a supernatural activity which requires the grace of God, and grace depends in large measure on our dispositions, the better these dispositions as we begin to pray the more assurance there is that our prayer will be successful. St. Ignatius repeatedly directs the one giving the Exercises to attend to this preparation, which guarantees to make prayer not only externally satisfactory but spiritually efficacious. He says more about the remote preparation and less about the

proximate because he assumes that the latter is not so necessary if the former has been faithfully done.

The first requisite for deriving maximum profit from the
Spiritual Exercises (or any form of prayer) is to have the exercitant "enter upon them with a large heart and liberality toward his Creator and Lord, and to offer Him his entire will
and liberty, that His Divine Majesty may dispose of him and
all he possesses according to His most holy will."[1] The implicit
attitude is generosity of spirit and a willingness to be guided
by every light and inspiration that comes from God. Without
this submissiveness of will, God will either not give us the
graces we need or, if He gives them, they are sure to be resisted.

Besides the will, the mind must also be prepared by segrega-
tion from worldly thoughts and cares. "Ordinarily, the progress
made in the Exercises will be greater, the more the exercitant
withdraws from all friends and acquaintances and from all
earthly concerns."[2] As a plea for the closed retreat, with perfect silence, it is impossible to improve on this statement of
St. Ignatius. But the advantages given for seclusion can be
equally adduced in favor of prayer at any time. The basic advantage is that by such withdrawal a person "gains no little
merit before the Divine Majesty." Also the mind "is more free
to use its natural powers to seek diligently what it so much
desires." But most important is the need for proper dispositions to receive the grace of God, since "the more the soul is
in solitude and seclusion, the more fit it renders itself to approach and be united with its Creator and Lord. And the more
closely it is united with Him, the more it disposes itself to
receive graces and gifts from the infinite goodness of God."[3]

A practical suggestion that refers to morning meditation has
a solid foundation in human psychology. "After retiring, just
before falling asleep, for the space of a Hail Mary, I will think

[1] Annotation 5.
[2] Annotation 20.
[3] Ibid.

of the hour when I have to arise, and why I am rising, and briefly sum up the exercise I have to go through." After awaking, "I will not permit my thoughts to roam at random, but will turn my mind at once to the subject I am about to contemplate. . . . As I dress, I will think over these thoughts and others in keeping with the subject matter of the meditation."[4] As a matter of common experience the latest impressions of the mind just before sleep are the most likely to run in the mind upon rising. But especially the first thoughts in the morning can start a mental pattern for the rest of the day. Properly controlled and directed, here on a definite subject for prayer, they bring vigor and momentum to the subsequent meditation that could not otherwise be secured.

The immediate preparation for prayer is a momentary concentration of forces, bearing first on myself and then on God. Regarding self, I should recall what I am about to do, "where I am going . . . what I must do"; regarding God, I should become conscious "in whose presence I am." Ignatius even suggests a small ritual: "I will stand for the space of an Our Father, a step or two before the place where I am to meditate or contemplate, and with my mind raised on high, consider that God our Lord beholds me. Then I will make an act of reverence or humility."[5] Apparently insignificant, this preliminary action along with reverent posture substantially contributes to more effective prayer. There is an influence of mind on body and vice versa: the sincerity of my internal sentiments appears in bodily form, and the body reinforces my internal sentiments.

THREE STAGES IN MENTAL PRAYER

A key to the proper understanding of St. Ignatius' teaching on prayer is the triple division he makes in the spiritual faculties of man: his memory, understanding and will. These are the "three powers of the soul" which figure so prominently

---

[4] *Additions for the First Week*, nn. 1–2.
[5] *Ibid.*, num. 3.

throughout the Exercises and in one form or another enter into the body of every meditation. Another and more important feature is the stress on prayer of petition which introduces, ends and surrounds the Exercises like an atmosphere and gives them a quality distinctive of Ignatian spirituality.

As a person begins to meditate, he makes a request of God our Lord, "that all my intentions, actions and operations may be directed solely to the praise and service of His Divine Majesty." Unexpectedly this preparatory prayer "must always be the same, without any alteration," even where the rest of the meditation is completely changed.

The Preludes are related to the body of a meditation somewhat as an author's preface introduces a book or a topic sentence the paragraph. They summarize in outline the contents of what follows.

On examination we find that some of the Exercises have two preludes and others three; but their function never changes. When three preludes are prescribed, the first is a review by the memory, when I "call to mind the history of the matter which I have to contemplate"; the second an image for the mind or "composition of place," on which to focus attention; and the third an act of the will, "to ask for what I want," as the special grace of this particular exercise. Generally the operations of memory and intellectual-phantasy are fused into one, so that only two preludes are required. The first will differ according to the subject matter. "In meditation on visible matters such as the contemplation of Christ our Lord, who is visible, the contemplation will be to see with the eyes of the imagination the corporeal place where the thing I wish to contemplate is found," e.g., the temple or mountain where Christ is preaching. "In meditation on invisible things," like the virtues and sins, some phantasm must still be created by the imagination on which the mind can fix attention. It may be a figurative representation of the spiritual reality in the manner of Christ's parables (the kingdom of heaven is like a treasure hidden in a field, the mercy of God represented by the Good

Shepherd), or at least a verbal expression in the interior senses, which somehow embodies the ideas that will form the structure of the meditation.

The last prelude is invariably an act of petition "to ask God our Lord for what I wish and desire."

Psychologically the preludes are indispensable. Unless I have something presented to the mind by the memory as a subject for prayer, I will have nothing to think about; with nothing prayerful in the mind to offer to the will, I will have nothing to petition for. Ordinarily the more definite the preludes the better, since they not only make the prayer get under way but keep it going by offering a specific object of attention (for the mind) and intention (for the will) to which I can always recur.

The Body of the Meditation or Contemplation elaborates on the preludes and follows the same sequence. Whatever the points, or whether even definite points are had, the three powers of the soul must be used to derive full profit from mental prayer. The memory furnishes material for the mind, either to contemplate or reason about; and the mind submits the fruit of its intuition or conclusions to the will for appropriate affections.

While all three powers must be operative, not all are equally important. Better for the mind to have a new thought or derive a conclusion than for the memory (aided by the imagination) to parade a variety of objects before the mind. Most important is the function of the will by which I express my desires, hopes and fears to God, according to the good and bad things recognized by the mind.

Recognizing an objective value-difference in the three functions, there should be a parallel difference in using the historical (or imaginative) memory, the intellect and will. The least time and effort should be given to the memory. Thus in the first regular meditation of the Exercises, St. Ignatius instructs the retreatant "to apply the memory to the first sin, which was that of the angels, and then *immediately* to employ the understanding on the same by turning it over in the mind."

There is no prescription on how much time or effort should be given to the operations of the mind. This will depend a great deal on the character and temperament of the person praying. Ascetical writers distinguish two kinds of people in their approach to prayer. One class is naturally more analytic, given to reasoning and penetrating to the ultimate causes of things. Consistent with their temperament, they have the option of dwelling on the discursive operations as much as they need to arouse the movements of the will. Other people are more spontaneously drawn to volition, either because their minds are not discursive or because their mental insights come in flashes and stimulate the will in repeated sequence. The relative emphasis on the use of the mind also depends on the kind of subject matter proposed for prayer. St. Ignatius has two principal forms, covered by the terms "meditation" and "application of the senses." The former is more of an intellectual operation which busies itself in reasoning and is altogether of a higher order. It inquires into the causes of the mysteries and their effects. It investigates God's attributes, His goodness, wisdom and love. The sense-application does not reason (or hardly so), but merely reposes in sense manifestations of sight, hearing and the rest.

Athough active in both cases, the reasoning process becomes minimal in sense-application, either because "the mind is unfit for more profound speculation" or because "the soul is already so filled with devotion obtained from former penetration into the deeper mysteries" that the slightest stimulus from the internal senses can excite the spiritual appetite.[6]

An often-quoted passage of St. Ignatius declares, "It is not much knowledge that fills and satisfies the soul, but the intimate understanding and relish of the truth."[7] This is not a platitude. He does not say that affection is better than mere

---

[6] *Monumenta Historica*, "Exercitia Spiritualia," p. 1150.
[7] *Introductory Observations*, II.

knowledge, which no one would question. Rather he compares two kinds of apprehension of religious truth, both knowledge in their way; but the one is quantitative and the other qualitative. The one may be had by a learned theologian or scholar, the other lies open to the pure of heart who can see God. They correspond to the notional and real assent of Cardinal Newman, where the same revealed truths in one case are merely adhered to, and in the other so deeply realized that they permeate the whole man and affect all his operations.

Running as a theme through the Exercises is the dominant role given to the will in every kind of prayer, as the logical terminus to the acts of memory and understanding. Naturally there are commanded acts of the will throughout the process, because unless I want to use my mind in spiritual reflection I will not do so. But the elicited acts of love and desire, of hope and petition are what technically constitutes formal prayer. For many reasons, a person should concentrate on these as much as he can.

Elicited acts of the will are normally of greater merit, as seen in the discussion of the Kingdom of Christ, because they involve greater voluntariety.

If too much time and energy is given to the use of the memory and intelligence, there may be "exhaustion" of the spiritual powers in the allotted time of prayer and consequently the will is not employed to its normal capacity.

Since the ultimate fruit of prayer is the love of God which terminates in generous service, unless the will be duly motivated in the time of formal prayer, the affections are lacking in necessary strength to carry one's charity into constant, self-sacrificing effect. In this context St. Ignatius sets a hierarchy of emphasis among the three powers of the soul for their use in prayer. He instructs the retreatant "to bring to memory" the history or picture as the subject of meditation, "then in turn to reason *more in particular* with the understanding, and thus in turn to move *still more* the affections by means of the will." Once the will is deeply affected, it has only to command the other powers of mind and body and there follows a complete dedication to the service of God.

Colloquies or acts of the will should be made throughout, but especially at the close of prayer, according to Ignatius' directives for every meditation of the retreat. "The colloquy is made properly by speaking as one friend speaks to another, or as a servant to his master; at one time *asking* for some favor, at another blaming oneself for some evil committed, now informing him of one's affairs, and *seeking* counsel in them."[8] To be noted is the characteristic Ignatian petition for grace which envelops the meditations, from the preludes at the beginning of the Exercises to the colloquy at the end.

Perhaps the outstanding (and most outspoken) authority on the subject was St. Alphonsus Liguori, patron of spiritual directors, who called the Spiritual Exercises the touchstone of a successful apostolate. He is writing on the importance of the prayer of petition:

What most afflicts me is to see preachers and confessors paying so little attention in speaking to their listeners and penitents of this kind of prayer. To what purpose, I ask, are sermons, meditations and the rest, except to produce spiritual harm, without prayer, when the Lord has declared that He does not will to give graces except to one who prays, "Ask and you shall receive." Without prayer, speaking of the ordinary providence, all the meditations made, promises and resolutions taken, remain useless. For if we do not pray, we shall ever be unfaithful to the lights we receive from God and the promises that we make. The reason is that actually to do good, to overcome temptation, to exercise virtue, in a word, entirely to keep the Divine precepts, it is not enough to receive lights and make reflections and resolutions; we still need the actual help of God. And the Lord does not grant this actual aid except to one who prays and prays with perseverance.[9]

The simplest proof for the need of asking for divine grace is the experience of those who pray. Their acquired strength of

8 *Ibid.*, Colloquy.
9 St. Alphonsus Liguori, *Opere Ascetiche*, Vol. II, Torino, 1877, p. 516.

soul to resist temptation and grow in the love of God are an expression of the law of sanctity.

But Ignatian colloquies serve another function than to concentrate our requests of God. Fundamentally they are conlocutions, personal interchanges of thought and intention between the soul and her Creator. As such they transcend the immediate purpose of the Exercises and represent one of the easiest ways of fulfilling the injunction of praying always. As long as I engage in conscious dialogue with the invisible world, the material subject of my colloquy is secondary. It may be a sublime mystery like the Trinity or the hypostatic union, or only a trifle like the pattern for a veil that Teresa of Avila made the subject of so much prayer. What is most important is my active conversation with Jesus Christ, the Blessed Virgin or one of the saints, with whom I unite myself in will and aspiration and to whom I address the sentiments of my heart.

Colloquies embody a radical principle of Catholic theology, namely, the concept of mediation in the economy of grace. In all the critical meditations of the retreat, Ignatius urges the exercitant to make a triple colloquy, beginning with the Blessed Virgin and ending with the eternal Father. Thus after the meditation on personal sin, I make a "colloquy to Our Lady that she may obtain for me grace from her Son and Lord for three things: that I may feel an interior knowledge of my sins . . . that I may feel the deordination of my actions in order to amend and order myself aright . . . and to beg for a knowledge of the world, so that, abhorring it, I may put away from myself worldly and vain things." Then a second colloquy to the Son, "that He may obtain for me from the Father the same grace." And finally a petition to the Eternal Lord, "that He may grant the same requests to me." Always the first colloquy is with Mary, whose dignity as mediatrix of graces is graphically professed when I begin by asking her to intercede with her divine Son for what I need. In like manner the mediation of Christ with His heavenly Father is duly recognized and the function of His human nature as the instrument of our salva-

tion are properly conceived. This double accent on the media-
torial role of Mary with Jesus and of Christ with His Father
was not accidental, as other writings of St. Ignatius clearly indicate. It was a spontaneous reaction against the Protestant
de-emphasis of Mary's place in the scheme of redemption and
a restatement of the Church's teaching on Christ's humanity
as the channel of grace in the Christian dispensation.

THREE METHODS OF PRAYER

Unless properly understood, the Three Methods of Prayer
may suffer from one of two extremes: being neglected as a
mere appendix, or identified with St. Ignatius' whole doctrine
on prayer. They are neither. Their aim was to supplement the
basic method of prayer elaborated in the meditations and contemplations of the Exercises, while including a number of
points of asceticism that apply to every form of prayer.

Actually these methods are only to serve as models to the
retreatants. "It must not be thought that other methods are
excluded, which the Holy Spirit is accustomed to teach; which
are commonly recognized by authorities on the spiritual life
as conformable to sound doctrine, right reason and human
psychology; or which anyone from personal experience has
found useful for his own progress in virtue."[10]

While immediately adapted to persons who are less profi-
cient in the science of prayer, the Three Methods are by no
means limited to such people, and everyone, no matter how
advanced in the spiritual life, can use them to advantage.

The First Method is a practical reflection on the commandments of God and the Church, the capital sins, the three powers of the soul and the five senses. Not otherwise than in
formal meditation, we have a preparatory prayer and a final
colloquy. In between is the actual method. Going in sequence
from one commandment or faculty to the next, I *briefly* consider whether and where I have been deficient. If there are
defects, I ask for pardon and the grace to amend myself in the

[10] *Monumenta*, p. 1074.

future. The general structure approximates the General Examen of Conscience, with its five points of gratitude, prayer for light and strength, examination, prayer for pardon and a purpose of amendment. But there are two important differences. The purpose is not so much to discover one's sins in the immediate past as to arouse sentiments of humility and gratitude from reflecting on my infidelity to God and His merciful love towards me. Also unlike a strict examination of conscience, the first method calls for meditation on the virtues, "in order to understand better the faults committed . . . and acquire and retain the virtues" opposed to the contrary sins. To this end, as a person wishes to imitate, e.g., the Blessed Virgin in her use of the senses, "he should recommend himself to her in the preparatory prayer that she obtain for him this grace from her Son, and after the consideration of each sense say a Hail Mary."

The Second Method differs from the first which looks primarily to moral or ascetical improvement. Primarily dogmatic, it seeks to deepen one's understanding of the Catholic faith. The Spanish autograph describes it as a "*contemplation* on the *meaning* of each word of a prayer," which may be the Apostles' Creed, the Pater Noster, or any other formulary rich in doctrinal content.

Externally the method is simplicity itself, calling for meditation on each word or phrase in sequence, "as long as a person finds various meanings, comparisons, relish and consolation in the consideration of it." But radically, it means concentrating all the forces at our command to obtain that conviction about the truths of revelation which forms the basis of Christian perfection. In the last century, the Vatican Council canonized the method by a solemn definition on how to penetrate into the mysteries of God:

If human reason, with faith as its guide, inquires earnestly, devoutly and circumspectly, it reaches, by God's generosity, a most profitable understanding of mysteries. This is accomplished by finding similarity with truths which are naturally known, and by seeing the relationship of mysteries with one another and with the final end of man.[11]

Here as elsewhere in the Exercises, St. Ignatius points up the value of depth and intensity over mere quantity, so that "if in contemplation on the Our Father, a person finds in one or two words abundant matter for thought, and much relish and consolation, he should not be anxious to go on, though the whole hour be taken up with what he has found."[12] At least at the end of prayer, the mind should be directed away from the mystery or truth under reflection, and "turn to the person to whom the prayer is directed, asking for the virtues or graces that are seen to be most needed."[13] By implication, therefore, all through the meditation on some truth of revelation, there was personal contact between the one praying and God or one of His saints in whose company the considerations were made.

The Third Method is a set of practical directives peculiarly suited to improving the recitation of vocal prayers. They are to develop "a habit of saying our vocal prayers with attention and devotion. . . . Hence this practice is very useful for those who are under obligation of reciting the canonical hours or other (non-liturgical) vocal prayers," such as the Litanies and the Rosary.[14]

Practically, the method consists in correlating a rhythmic period of time, e.g., between breaths or longer if preferred, with reflection on some spiritual truth which may be only extrinsically connected with the words of the prayer. St. Ignatius suggests four possibilities: during a short "space of time, the attention is chiefly directed to the meaning of the word (or phrase being vocalized), to the person who is addressed, to our

---

[11] Denzinger, 1796.
[12] *Second Method of Prayer*, Rule 2.
[13] *Ibid.*, Note 2.
[14] *Monumenta*, p. 1174.

own lowliness, or the difference between the dignity of the person and our own insignificance."

Treating of the same subject, St. Thomas gives three ways of making vocal prayer attentive: "Pay attention to the words spoken, not to mispronounce them; or reflect on the meaning of the words themselves; or, what is most necessary, recognize the end for which the prayer is said, while directing the mind to God or to the intention for which we pray. Even ordinary people are capable of this latter method which, on occasion, makes the mind so intent upon God as to become oblivious of everything else."[15] Except for the more technical terminology, this is substantially the teaching of the Exercises.

However implemented or applied, St. Ignatius' third method is calculated to meet the most serious problem in vocal prayer —how to keep the mind from wandering. The solution he offers is realistic. As long as the mind is somehow alert to what it is doing, there is food for the will and the action is a genuine prayer.

---

[15] St. Thomas, *Summa Theologica*, IIa IIae, q. 83, a. 13.

11

Mysteries of the Life of Christ

THE solid core of the Spiritual Exercises, around which everything else revolves, is the set of fifty mysteries of the life of Christ normally placed after the key meditations and consequently liable to be taken as an after-thought instead of something essential to an Ignatian retreat. But whenever the Exercises are made for five or more days, most of the meditations will be given on the life of Christ. St. Ignatius' choice of mysteries, therefore, and the special emphasis which he gives them are of primary importance in setting the tone and giving orientation to any retreat where the reflections have not been reduced to the absolute minimum.

In the following analysis we shall not undertake to comment on the mysteries in detail, but rather evaluate the master ideas that dominate what looks to the inexperienced eye like an itemized list of passages from the Gospels, chosen at random and arbitrarily strung together into sets of three unrelated points.

The first salient feature of these mysteries is their vitalism. Ignatius had a large area of Scripture texts to choose from; by actual count over twenty-five hundred verses, exclusive of duplications, in the Gospels alone. In adapting this vast material he made a point of choosing mysteries that are best suited for the delicate synthesis of meditation and contemplation as recommended in the Exercises. In varying degree, he makes each mystery a dramatic episode, involving more than one person in communication or conflict and not just a static portrait or

monologue. There are people to see and hear in action, and
events are taking place in which the exercitant can participate
with all the faculties of body and mind—all directed to the
unique purpose of knowing Christ more intimately in order to
love Him more fervently and serve Him more faithfully. The
first and last of the fifty mysteries may serve as illustrations.

Annunciation of Our Lady

1. The Angel St. Gabriel, saluting our Lady, announced to
her the Conception of Christ our Lord. "And the Angel being
come in said unto her: 'Hail, full of grace . . . Behold thou
shalt conceive in thy womb, and shalt bring forth a Son.' "

2. The Angel confirms what he had said to our Lady by
announcing the conception of St. John the Baptist, saying to
her: "And behold thy cousin Elizabeth, she also hath conceived a son in her old age."

3. Our Lady replied to the Angel: "Behold the handmaid of
the Lord, be it done unto me according to thy word."

Here we see all the essential elements of the Annunciation
taken out of the Gospel of St. Luke and exhibited for concentrated meditation with perfect clarity. First the angelic message announcing with ecstatic suddenness the fulfillment of
the messianic prophecies in the person of the Virgin Mary;
then the sign of Christ's miraculous conception by the parallel
miracle of Elizabeth bearing a child in her old age; finally, the
Incarnation itself, when Mary pronounces her consent to become the mother of God. Thus in a few words the main features of the mystery are delineated, like the few strokes of an
artist's pencil sketching the outline of a future painting. With
nothing essential missing, enough details are furnished to suggest both the general pattern and how the entire composition
needs to be developed.

Ascension of Christ our Lord

1. After Christ our Lord had shown Himself for forty days

to the Apostles, "giving many proofs and signs . . . and speaking of the Kingdom of God," He commanded them to await in Jerusalem the Holy Spirit He had promised them.

2. He led them forth to Mount Olivet, and in their presence "He was raised up, and a cloud received Him out of their sight."

3. While they are looking up to Heaven angels say to them, "Ye men of Galilee, why stand you looking up to Heaven? This Jesus, Who is taken up from you into Heaven, shall so come as you have seen Him going into Heaven."

Again the same genius for reducing to miniature the whole sweep of an extended mystery, enabling the mind to penetrate with a single glance to the essence of the closing events of Christ's visible stay upon earth. After appearing for forty days with many proofs of His bodily resurrection He told the Apostles to wait in Jerusalem for the coming of the Holy Spirit He had promised them. On the fortieth day He rose from the midst of His disciples into heaven on the same Mount Olivet where shortly before He had suffered His agony in the garden. Then the closing angelic announcement, not unlike the first one at Nazareth, that Jesus who came down from heaven as God and ascended into heaven as the God-man, will return on the last day as the Son of Man to judge the living and the dead. Thus in less than one hundred words we are given a synthesis of the crowning event in the life of Christ, at the point where the Incarnation becomes a double test of our faith, that the Spirit which Christ sent animates the Church whose Mystical Head is the living Son of God in human flesh.

INTERPRETATION AND EXTRA SCRIPTURAL DETAILS

St. Ignatius is properly regarded as one of the Church's greatest mystics, whose life, from the time of his conversion at Loyola, was a series of heavenly visitations that gave him a profound insight into the truths of the Christian religion. In the process of canonization, the cardinal postulator for the cause of St. Ignatius testified that the Blessed Virgin alone appeared more than thirty times to Inigo during the eight months of his first retreat at Manresa. Ignatius himself supplies further details when confidentially describing his experiences during those early days when the Spiritual Exercises were born:

Often in prayer, [he said], and even during a long space of time, did he see the humanity of Christ with the eyes of the soul. The form under which this vision appeared was that of a white body, neither large nor small; besides, there seemed to be no other distinction of members in His body. This vision appeared to him often at Manresa, perhaps twenty or even forty times. . . . He saw the Blessed Virgin under the same form, without any distinction of members. These visions gave him such strength that he often thought within himself, that even though Scripture did not bear witness to these mysteries of faith, still, from what he had seen, it would be his duty to lay down his life for them.[1]

It is not surprising, therefore, that while keeping very close to the text of the New Testament, Ignatius more than once makes a personal interpretation or adds a significant detail that suggests divine illumination. But even as purely natural *obiter dicta*, they are valuable aids to a deeper understanding of the Exercises.

In the Annunciation, the angel Gabriel reportedly "confirms what he had said to our Lady by announcing the conception of John the Baptist." This is an informative gloss on the passage in St. Luke since Mary, otherwise than Zachary, did not ask for a miraculous sign as a condition for belief. Yet Ignatius so interprets Elizabeth's conception in her old age and thus highlights an important factor in the criteriology of faith, that even the faith of the Blessed Virgin could profit from having a truth of revelation confirmed by external miracle.

After the Circumcision of Christ, those who performed the rite "return the Child to His Mother, who felt compassion at the blood shed by her Son." It would be a mistake to suppose that this was only a dramatic touch to focus attention on the

[1] *The Autobiography of St. Ignatius*, New York, 1900, p. 56.

Blessed Virgin's sympathy for the Child Jesus. St. Ignatius was too restrained in literary composition for us to doubt that he had some higher reason for the addition. Even if the reference to Mary's compassion was not the result of a private inspiration, it fits in perfectly with the Mariology of the Exercises. The role of mediatrix between Christ and mankind is characteristic of Ignatian spirituality. But if Mary is mediatrix, she must have earned this title by her close association in spirit with the redemptive sufferings of her divine Son—not only in the Passion and under the cross but from the first time that He shed His blood in obedience to the will of His Father manifested through the Mosaic law.

In line with the same concept of mediation, when Jesus enters on His public life, He "takes leave of His Blessed Mother," where the mutual pain of separation is specified at the very moment when Christ began the final stage of our salvation. Since a generous retreat election may require the sacrifice of family ties and consolations for the sake of the Gospel, this episode may serve as an example of how Christ and His Mother should be imitated if we would be perfect and offer "gifts of greater than ordinary worth" for the love of God.

And again at the marriage feast of Cana, Ignatius takes the liberty of changing two verbs in the Gospel story, to highlight the authority that Mary has as our mediator with Christ. The evangelist relates simply that Mary "says to Jesus" that the wine has run out, and that she "says to the attendants" to do whatever Jesus will direct. But in the Exercises, Mary does not merely tell Jesus, she *points out* to Him that the wine has run short; and she *orders* the waiters to follow the instructions of Christ. As told by St. Ignatius, the mystery shows Mary taking the whole initiative, from recognizing that the wine had given out to commanding that her Son's directives should be promptly obeyed.

When *driving the sellers* out of the temple, Jesus acts somewhat differently towards the money changers and towards those who were selling doves. St. John says that He overturned the tables of the former and told the latter to "take these things hence and do not make the house of my Father a house of business." St. Ignatius adds two pertinent details. He describes the money changers as rich and the sellers of doves as poor, and according to him Jesus spoke mildly to the poor merchants but angrily to the others. For any one else it might have been only a trivial detail, but, considering the insistence on poverty throughout the Exercises, the overt distinction in this mystery between the rich and the poor and the different attitude of Christ towards each was scarcely indeliberate.

The Passion and Death of Christ include a number of revealing interpretations and additions. In the agony in the garden, St. Luke relates that Christ sweated blood which ran down upon the ground. From this St. Ignatius concludes that the flow of blood must have been copious and "supposes that His garments were already full of blood"; otherwise how explain the running down from the body onto the ground? And if the flow of blood was so copious, how intense must have been the agony to produce it?

During the terrible night in the house of Caiphas, when the soldiers mocked the Savior, blindfolded and buffeted Him, St. Ignatius adds that "in a thousand other ways they blasphemed Him," which is nowhere directly alluded to in the sacred text.

On the way to Calvary, the three synoptics tell us that the soldiers prevailed on Simon of Cyrene to carry the cross after Jesus. But they do not give the reason. According to Ignatius, it was because the pain and fatigue were beyond endurance; "as He could not carry it, Simon of Cyrene was forced to carry it after Jesus."

After the crucifixion, the Gospel narrative tells how Joseph of Arimathea asked for the body of Jesus and took it down from the cross. John adds the information that Nicodemus came with a mixture of myrrh and aloes and, together with Joseph, buried Jesus. But St. Ignatius states that both Joseph and Nicodemus took Jesus down from the cross and adds, "in the presence of His sorrowful Mother." He therefore implies that Mary remained with her Son on the cross to the very end, the valiant woman who shared in His sufferings and along with Him cooperated in the redemption of mankind.

Christ's first appearance after the resurrection to His Blessed Mother is taken for granted. For although not mentioned in Scripture, if He appeared to many others besides the few named, it is clear that among these His Mother was the most worthy and therefore the first to be consoled by His risen humanity. All the known sources that Ignatius consulted took the fact for granted, as Suarez explains in commenting on this mystery. "There is not the slightest doubt that after the resurrection, Christ appeared to His Mother before anyone else. This is so intrinsically credible as to be almost universally accepted by the great doctors of the Church, the faithful in general and by all Catholic writers who touch upon the subject." When Mark says that Christ "appeared first to Mary Magdalen," this should be taken to mean either that she was the first among those whom the Gospels describe as witnesses of the resurrection or among those to whom Christ appeared in order to confirm their faith. Hence the omission of any reference to the Blessed Virgin.[2]

In the apparition at Emmaus, St. Ignatius states without apology that Christ was recognized when He consecrated the Eucharistic elements and gave Holy Communion to the two disciples. The author of the Exercises was here following the teaching of many of the Fathers who, like St. Augustine, saw in Christ's revelation of Himself at Emmaus an expression of the common law of Christianity that "no one should be considered as really knowing Christ, unless he is a member of His body, which is the Church, whose unity in the Sacrament of Bread is described by the Apostle when he says, because the Bread is one, we though many, are one Body."[3]

Other appearances of Christ, not narrated in the Gospels but included in the Exercises, are the apparition to Joseph of

2 Francis Suarez, *De Mysteriis Vitae Christi,* Disp. XLIX, sec. 1, num. 2.
3 St. Augustine, "De Consensu Evangelistarum," PL 34, 1206.

Arimathea, His descent into Limbo where "He appeared in spirit to the holy fathers," and His frequent appearance to the disciples during the forty days before the ascension. Since Joseph of Arimathea was so closely associated with Christ during life and in death, it seems only natural that the Lord should have favored him with a personal visitation. The descent into Limbo is an article of faith, taught by the early Church and incorporated in the Creed at least since the fourth century. The appearance "many times to the disciples" amplifies St. Paul's statement to the Corinthians that the Risen Savior was seen by more than five hundred of the brethren and by all the apostles. Thus stated without hesitation and without the qualification "as may piously be believed," we may suppose it was the fruit of a divine communication.

AREAS OF SPECIAL CONCENTRATION

Although St. Ignatius makes a fairly complete coverage of Christ's life in the mysteries that he chooses, there are certain aspects which he favors more than others, certain omissions and an obvious concentration in certain areas which deserve to be better known as revealing the mind of the author of the Exercises.

The Divinity of Christ is the first cardinal mystery which Ignatius emphasizes. At the beginning of His public life, during the baptism in the Jordan, a heavenly voice proclaims Jesus the beloved Son of the Father. Immediately after, during the temptation in the desert, the devil tries to test the divinity of Christ. He fails, but the lesson is impressed on the readers of the Gospel narrative. In the sermon on the mount, Christ proclaims His superiority to the law of Moses and His equality with the Lord of the Mosaic code. In the transfiguration He appears between Moses and Elias as the fulfillment of their prophecies. After the resurrection, He accepts the confession of St. Thomas, "My Lord and my God," and just before the ascension declares that all power was given to Him in heaven and on earth.

Then in attestation of these claims to divinity, Christ works miracles of transcendent power: changing water into wine at Cana, calming the storm at sea and walking on the water, multiplying the loaves and fishes, and raising Lazarus from the grave. Significantly, of all the forty miracles recorded in the Gospels, St. Ignatius chooses only these, prodigies of power over nature which bows in obedience to her Creator. By contrast not a single healing narrative occurs among the mysteries of Christ's life in the Exercises.

St. Ignatius' preoccupation with the divinity of Christ is not accidental. It places the humanity of the Son of God in proper focus and gives it a dogmatic foundation without which the following of Christ would be only devotion to a great leader or dedication to a great cause. It would not be the imitation and service of God in human flesh.

Throughout the Exercises, the retreatant learns to know Christ more intimately in order to love Him more ardently in order to serve Him more faithfully. The knowledge of Christ, therefore, is the basis of Christian perfection and the measure of all our holiness. We cannot serve with genuine fidelity unless we love and we cannot love unless we know. But what does it mean to know Christ? What is there to know about Him and what kind of knowledge do we have? The answer to these questions cuts so deeply into the science of theology that it separates the whole Christian world into two camps, those who possess the true faith and those who do not. And among true believers, it distinguishes those who live only on the surface of Christianity from those who have penetrated to its depths.

To know Christ certainly means to know the man who was born at Bethlehem and during life was revered as a prophet until He was murdered by the Jewish leaders who envied His successful preaching and resented His exposing their hypocrisy. It means to know all that the Gospels relate about Jesus of Nazareth, His miracles and teaching and all the events that are recorded about the man whose thirty short years have revolutionized the history of mankind. This kind of knowledge, however, may be only information which even a pagan or un-believer can have, or, at best, a sublimated form of earthly wisdom which sees in Christ perhaps the greatest teacher that the world has ever known and a paragon of all the virtues. But this is not what St. John describes in the prologue of his Gospel, that the Word was made flesh and dwelt among us, or what St. Paul means when he writes about the Image of the invisible God, in whom were created all things in the heavens and on the earth.

An adequate knowledge of Christ comprehends not only His humanity but especially His divinity. It sees with the eyes of faith, illumined by grace, that the man Jesus was the incarnate Son of God, and as a consequence His every human action which affects my life takes on a new dimension. The virtues of patience, humility, and poverty that I seek to imitate are theandric perfections that reveal the Word become flesh, and the kindness and mercy to which I am attracted are the Infinite Goodness in human form. The mysteries of faith that I am asked to believe and the commandments I am told to observe, both beyond the capacity of nature to understand or obey, are made credible and possible because the human being who proclaims them has the wisdom and authority of God.

If I consider the Church which Christ established, I see it is not only a juridical organization but a Mystical Body animated by the divine Spirit of its founder. The result is a sense of nearness to Christ for which no earthly substitute can be found. Removed from its bare historical setting, the Incarnation enters into perspective as the eternal union of God with human nature, physically in the person of Christ and mystically in the *totus Christus* of which I, as a member of the Mystical Body, am an integral part. Indeed, Christ Himself, personally present in the Church, gives us the highest motive for loving the Society which He directs as its living Head. "For it is Christ who lives in the Church, and through her teaches, governs and sanctifies."[4] But all of this becomes possible only because Christ is God.

So, too, the sacraments take on a deeper meaning in the light of Christ's divinity. They are seen not only as external signs which He instituted to be the instruments of grace but as seven channels through which His redemptive blood flows in a constant stream, like so many arteries, to impart, sustain and increase the supernatural life of the cells in the Mystical Body. For although Christ originated the sacraments during His visible stay upon earth, as the divine Author of grace He is perennially active in every sacramental ritual where He directly exercises His almighty power for the sanctification of souls.

The Kindness and Mercy of Christ are nicely balanced with the power of His divinity by a judicious choice of those mysteries which picture the Saviour as acquainted with our infirmities and more willing to help us than we are to ask for His aid. By His temptation in the desert, He showed us how perfectly human He was, being like to us in all things except sin, and how intrinsic to human nature are trials and temptations, from which even the Son of God was not exempt. He can therefore sympathize with our own sufferings and probation as one who had the same experience. At the wedding feast in Cana, His solicitude for the guests when the wine had failed shows the range of Christ's interest in everything that concerns us, not excluding our temporal welfare and including the amenities of bodily comfort.

In the sermon on the mount, in addition to the beatitudes of meekness, mercy and peaceableness, Ignatius directs our attention to Christ's exhortation that we love our enemies and do good to them that hate us, in the spirit of the Lord's Prayer, "forgive us our trespasses as we forgive those who trespass against us." This concept, according to a Hebrew scholar, of asking forgiveness of God in return for mercy towards man is

[4] Pius XII, Encyclical *Mystici Corporis Christi*, N.C.W.C. Translation, 1943, p. 36.

foreign to Jewish theology, and adds a new principle to social morality.[5] It required the example and teaching of incarnate Love to propose the idea and make it the hallmark of Christian perfection.

At least two miracles of Christ which Ignatius makes into separate meditations are designed to encourage our confidence in His care for us and under no circumstances to distrust Him. During the storm at sea, when the terrified disciples awakened Christ, He reproved their "little faith" and then commanded the winds and the sea to be still. Again on the Lake of Galilee, when Peter at Christ's bidding walked upon the water and then "hesitating" began to sink, the Lord took him by the hand but reproachfully asked him, "You of little faith, why did you doubt?" In both mysteries, the original word for "faith" comes from the Greek *pistis*, which the evangelists regularly use to describe the confidence in Christ's power and mercy that He required of those in whose favor He worked miracles. "Daughter," He said to the woman with the flux of blood, "your faith [*pistis*] has made you whole." And "because of their unbelief [*pistis*], He did not work many miracles there" in Nazareth.

St. Ignatius, following the more common tradition, identifies the sinful woman in Luke's Gospel with Mary of Magdala, and entitles the meditation "the conversion of Magdalen." Commentators since patristic times have regarded this mystery as the classic example of Christ's mercy and suggested that it was preserved specially for the gentiles (through St. Paul's disciple) to prove that Christianity is the religion of love. Characteristically, Ignatius also transmits the problem of reconciling Christ's parable on that occasion with its application to the sinful woman. In the parable, the remission of debt becomes the source of grateful love; but applied to the woman, her love is described as the cause of forgiveness. Ignatius omits the parable and isolates the application, thus giving greater force to

[5] Felix Levy, *Universal Jewish Encyclopedia*, Vol. VII, p. 193.

the words of Christ which he quotes, "Many sins are forgiven her, because she has loved much." In other words, her extraordinary manifestation of love shows how well she recognized the debt of gratitude that was owed to the mercy of Christ.

For the benefit of those working in the apostolate, Ignatius singled out a mystery where the understanding sympathy of Christ is contrasted with a certain callousness on the part of the disciples. They suggested He dismiss the crowd that was following Him, since "this is a desert place and the hour is already late." But the Saviour did not listen to them. Instead he told ("commanded," says Ignatius) the disciples to bring some loaves and fishes and proceeded to feed the multitude of five thousand, not counting the women and children. The striking feature of this miracle, like the one at Cana, is its "superfluity." Immediately after feeding the people, Christ dismissed them; so there was no question of supplying food to sustain them for more instruction but only as a convenience to relieve their hunger before they came home. This was an object lesson for the followers of Christ in their dealings with souls, to extend their charity to every need they find, whether bodily or purely spiritual, essential or even dispensable.

The Call and Duties of the Apostolate are prominently featured, with an obvious aim to instruct those who are teaching or preaching the word of God. The longest single meditation among the fifty mysteries is on the "Vocation of the Apostles," where Ignatius distinguishes three stages in their calling to follow Christ. The first was "to some knowledge" of the Master, as described by the evangelist, John, which suggests the first step in the grace of an apostolic vocation. Christ invites a soul to learn more about Him and the redemptive purpose of His Incarnation. Then comes a further invitation to follow the Saviour more intimately, "with the intention of returning to what they had left," comparable to a temporary profession of vows or a transient commitment to Catholic Action. The final call is "to follow Christ our Lord forever," in a permanent dedication to His service. St. Ignatius therefore

recognized the divine strategy which begins by gently present-
ing the apostolic life as attractive in the person of Christ and
then by degrees leading a soul to consecrate itself for life to
the advancement of the Gospel.

Furthermore, "three other things are to be considered,"
which give us a rare insight into the nature of the apostolic vocation. We should reflect "how the Apostles were of a rude
and lowly condition," with nothing to recommend them except
their natural incompetence for the monumental task of estab-
lishing the Kingdom of God on earth. Yet it was precisely for
this reason, the ancient writers tell us, that Christ chose such
weak instruments, in order to manifest the supernatural character of His Church and forestall any suspicion that the society
which should one day surpass empires was the creation of human genius. In the same way, on the level of the apostolic
worker, Christ often chooses the least likely persons for the
work of evangelization and crowns their labor with phenome-
nal success, so that no flesh should glory in His sight. At the
other extreme, we are to consider "to what dignity the apostles
were so gently called." Elsewhere in his writings, St. Ignatius
was so impressed with the sublimity of the apostolate that he
allowed himself the rare liberty of describing it in extravagant
terms. "Not only not among men, but not even among the
angels can a more noble life be conceived than that of glorify-
ing God and of drawing creatures to Himself, so far as they
are capable of that attraction."[6] In spite of the grandeur of
this calling, however, or perhaps because of its sublimity, it
comes to the soul "gently" as an invitation to greater generosity and not as an imperative command. Between this dignity
of cooperating in the work of redemption and the natural im-
potence of the apostles stand "the gifts and graces by which
they were raised above the Fathers of the Old and New Testament" to become, in the words of St. Paul, the foundation of
the holy temple of God. As with the first evangelists, so with

[6] *Letters and Instructions of St. Ignatius*, London, 1914, p. 94.

their successors, the law of compensation must be operative. What nature cannot do becomes possible and easy through grace, to remind us that in the last analysis not we but the indwelling Spirit of Christ transforms sinners into saints and leads them from darkness to light through our ministrations.

Another meditation on the apostolate covers the mission that Christ gave to His chosen twelve, and through them to all who are dedicated to the spiritual welfare of their neighbor. Ignatius picked four qualities that characterized the ministry of the apostles, and by implication should characterize the work of their followers. On the injunction of Christ, the apostles were to be most prudent in their dealings with others, by acting with the wisdom of serpents and the simplicity of doves. Along with prudence, they were to be patient, since the Master foretold that He was sending them as sheep in the midst of wolves. Part of their patience was to be voluntary poverty, demanding no remuneration for their services, "Freely you have received, freely give," and taking no money for the journey but trusting in the support of providence. Finally the subject of their ministry was specified. They were to preach a spiritual message, the Kingdom of God, to which all material and secular interests were subordinate.

In all the voluminous instructions and correspondence that St. Ignatius wrote on the apostolic life, there is a special accent on the virtues of prudence, patience and poverty, and a constant insistence on the priority of spiritual values. Each of these elements was seen as a balance between opposite extremes: prudence as a counterpoise to thoughtless indiscretion and over-calculation; patience as a middle course to reluctant endurance and passive quietism; poverty concerned to promote a successful apostolate while imitating the poor Saviour who had not whereon to lay His head; and above all a supernatural realism that places union with Christ and the sources of grace above human effort and ability, but without despising any of the natural means that may advance the Kingdom of God. When Ignatius warned "the apostolic man not (to) for-

get himself; he has not come to handle gold but mud. He cannot therefore watch himself too carefully that he may not
contract the leprosy of which he seeks to cure others"; or
"there is nothing of which apostolic men have more need than
interior recollection," he was only repeating the ideas he had
woven into the Spiritual Exercises.[7]

THE RESURRECTION OF CHRIST

The most striking feature in St. Ignatius' treatment of the
life of Christ is the attention he gives to the resurrection, apparently out of all proportion to the objective value of the
mystery. Where the resurrection narratives occupy only five
per cent of the total content of the Gospels, in the Spiritual
Exercises fourteen out of fifty mysteries deal exclusively with
the risen life of the Saviour. In order to have enough material
for this specialization, Ignatius develops a single passage from
Scripture into a separate meditation, like the apparitions to
James and the five hundred brethren; he also goes outside the
Gospels to the Acts and the Pauline Epistles for additional
subject matter, and even makes a meditation out of Christ's
appearance to Joseph of Arimathea, "as may piously be thought
and as we read in the lives of the saints." Clearly St. Ignatius
was preoccupied with the resurrection to a point that must
seem strange until we examine the full import of this mystery
in the economy of the redemption.

According to St. Thomas, to whom Ignatius was most devoted, the first purpose of the resurrection was to vindicate the
divine justice, which elevates those who humble themselves.
"Since Christ humiliated Himself even to the death of the
Cross out of love and obedience to God, He was therefore exalted by God even to His resurrection from the dead."[8] It is
this glorification of His risen humanity to which Christ refers
in the meditation on the Kingdom when He says, "My will is

[7] Xavier de Franciosi, *L'Esprit de Saint Ignace*, Paris, 1948, p. 46.
[8] *Summa Theologica*, III[a], q. 53, a. 1.

to conquer the whole world and all my enemies, and thus to enter into the glory of my Father."

The resurrection of Christ is also the great proof of His divinity and in that sense the keystone of our faith. During His mortal life Christ had often professed Himself to be God in human flesh. "The Father and I are one," He declared. In testimony of this claim He allowed Himself to be crucified, died, and by His own power arose from the dead; thus clearly manifesting that He was indeed the Resurrection and the Life, first in His own favor and then for all the rest of mankind. Without the divinity of Christ, confirmed by the miracle of Easter Sunday, the incarnation is a misnomer and the redemption a sham. "If Christ has not risen," says St. Paul, "vain then is our preaching," and vain all the ideals of Christianity as presented in the Exercises.

Besides confirming our faith in His divinity, Christ's resurrection gives the hope of our own restoration from the grave. As the first fruits of those who sleep, the Head of the Mystical Body became a pledge of immortality to His faithful members on the last day. In the context of the Kingdom meditation this is integral to the promise of Christ that those who follow Him in labor and suffering will also follow Him in glory. While only part of the reward, the glorification of our body after the example of Christ can be a powerful motive in the spiritual life. Since the control of bodily passions by "acting against sensuality and carnal desires" often demands a great deal of sacrifice, there should be a corresponding remuneration, not only for the soul but also for the body which shared in the earthly struggle. For the soul, this reward is the beatific vision; for the body, it is the resurrection which endows the sensible faculties with transcendent powers and inebriates them, in the words of revelation, with the torrent of God's pleasure.

Finally and most importantly the resurrection of Christ is the cause of our reinstatement in the friendship of God. In patristic terminology, it is the complement of our salvation. As the result of Adam's fall we were twice removed from divine love, once by reason of original sin that infected our human nature and once again by the loss of sanctifying grace that gave us a title to the vision of God. Accordingly, St. Paul distinguishes two stages in our restoration by the mercy of Christ. "Jesus our Lord," he says, "was delivered up for our sins, and rose again for our justification."[9] This concept of a distinction between the redemptive work of Christ's passion and His resurrection deserves to be better known. Two kinds of life were to be restored, as there were two kinds of death from which we had to be redeemed, the one bodily and the other spiritual. As the passion of Christ removed both forms of death, so His resurrection restored both forms of life. And "since the flesh is the instrument of His divinity, and since an instrument operates in virtue of the principal cause, our double resurrection, bodily and spiritual, is referred to Christ's bodily resurrection as the cause."[10] The great difference, of course, between the redemptive function of the passion and resurrection is that only the former was meritorious, "for the glorified Christ was no longer a wayfarer and so was not in a position to merit." Yet there are so many ways that the risen Saviour is the cause of our supernatural life that theologians speak of the resurrection as pertaining to the integrity of our redemption.

The influence of Christ in His glorified humanity is exercised most universally as Head of the Mystical Body, the Catholic Church, of which we are the actual members. "Who has reached more lofty heights," asks Pius XII, "than Christ the Man who, though born of the Immaculate Virgin, is the true and natural Son of God, and in virtue of His miraculous and glorious resurrection, a resurrection triumphant over death, has become the first-born of the dead?" Because Christ is so exalted, He alone by every right rules and governs the Church, not only visibly through His ministers, but directly and personally, and with an intimacy that beggars description. "As the nerves extend from the head to all parts of the human body,

9 Romans 4:25.
10 *Compendium Theologiae*, cap. 239.

giving them power of feeling and movement, so the Saviour communicates His strength and virtue to the Church, to enlighten the minds of the faithful and inspire them with generous desires. From Him streams into the body of the Church all the light which divinely illumines those who believe, and all the grace by which they are made holy according to His own sanctity."[11]

All sanctity begins with Christ, and therefore has Christ as its cause. For no act conducive to salvation can be placed unless it proceeds from Him, the God-Man, as its supernatural source. Grace and virtue flow from His divinity, through the glorified humanity, for the salvation of the world. If we grieve and do penance for our sins, and return to God with humble confidence in His mercy, it is because Christ is leading us. He is continually pouring out His gifts of wisdom, counsel, and fortitude. When the sacraments are administered—baptism, confirmation, and the rest—it is the risen Christ who produces their effect in our souls. On the altar, in the Sacrifice of the Mass, the oblation of Calvary is renewed because it is the same Priest and Victim who offered Himself on the cross. Only the manner of offering is different. On the cross it was a bloody sacrifice, "but on the altar, by reason of the glorified state of His human nature, death shall have no more dominion over Him, and so the shedding of His blood is impossible."[12] And in Holy Communion we receive the risen Saviour in all the perfection of His humanity, hypostatically united with the divinity which has conquered the grave and, according to the promise of Christ, is the stay of our spiritual life on earth and the hope of being raised up on the last day.

In the light of these implications of the resurrection, we cannot wonder that St. Ignatius gives so much attention to the glorious mysteries, even, so it seems, at the expense of the mortal life. He recognized a guiding norm in Christian asceticism, which he incorporated into the Exercises and practically

[11] *Mystici Corporis Christi*, p. 19.
[12] Pius XII, Encyclical *Mediator Dei*, N.C.W.C. Translation, 1948, p. 28.

implemented by his accent on the risen Saviour. Implicit in all the great meditations, it says that Christianity in its ultimate components is not a mere juridical structure but a living organism, and its highest motivation which produces saints and heroes is more than a body of precepts binding under pain of sin. It is a Personality, at once divine and human, that still lives because of the resurrection, not only as a memory but as the object of present history, indwelling in the hearts of those who love Him and destined to be possessed for all eternity.

12

Discernment of Spirits

THE Rules for the Discernment of Spirits reveal St. Ignatius as a diagnostician of the spiritual life, whose principles of analysis were born of the interior struggle he experienced at Loyola, which ended in his conversion and began his dedication to the service of God. They were further refined, also from experience, during the subsequent years of conflict with the powers of evil battling for the mastery of his soul and against the apostolic work he had launched to check the forces of the Protestant rebellion.

More than any single part of the Exercises, the Rules for Discernment are autobiographical. But they are of universal application because they embody those elements of asceticism without which the *militia Christiana* would be doomed to failure. In the spirit of the Exercises, they bring the Two Standards out of the realm of history into the private life of every sincere follower of Christ. Their primary function, however, is to serve as necessary means for making a right Election. Inevitably the exercitant will be agitated by contrary spirits in the course of the retreat. Unless he learns to distinguish between these opposing forces and knows how to overcome the devil and respond to the inspirations of God, he can scarcely make a good Election and, to that extent, will profit only minimally from the Spiritual Exercises.

St. Ignatius' Rules of Discernment presuppose three kinds of interior movements which a person may experience. The first type is produced by the person himself and arises from the innate powers of his own mind and affections. The other two are induced by intelligent powers outside the person, and may be good or evil. If good, the operating agent is God or one of His obedient spirits; if evil, it is the devil in some form or another.

Consequently two kinds of discernment are logically demanded in the spiritual life. We should be able to distinguish our native thoughts and sentiments from those produced by forces outside of ourselves, and among the latter know the difference between inspirations that originate with God and temptations which come from the devil. The first discernment is not so important because all our interior movements are subject to the influence of God and are never completely isolated from the contrary activity of the devil. On the other hand, it is highly practical to be able to judge between alien personalities operating on our minds and wills, and know how to resist the machinations of the evil spirit.

In speaking of "movements" in the soul, we can refer to those which precede a deliberate action of the will, those involved in the actual choice itself, and those which follow. The discernment of spirits most properly refers to the antecedent motions of mind and will which, in a sense, impel the appetitive faculties in the direction of good or evil. It makes a world of difference whether these impulses are from God or the devil. Without forcing the will, they solicit my consent, and consequently my decision, for or against a given impulse, will be objectively good or bad according as the spirit which suggested the choice was divine or diabolical. In a subordinate way, the movements which follow an act of human choice are also worth discriminating as valuable signs that my choice was correct or otherwise; if correct, to repeat and confirm the decision, if wrong to change or revoke what I had decided.

There are two sets of rules in the Exercises, fourteen and eight, respectively. The former are more suited to the purgative stage in the spiritual life; the latter more suitable for the Second Week, or the illuminative way. In practice, they are equally valid for any level of spirituality and afford an insight into spiritual experience which is more than coldly intellectual; its full discrimination requires the whole man, including his sentiments and affections. Also the rules do not pretend to give a complete analysis of our interior motions, but only "to some extent," to be supplemented by learning, prayer and personal experience.

UNDERLYING PRINCIPLES

Three elementary principles underlie the rules of St. Ignatius for the discernment of spirits. If these principles have been duly grasped, the rules themselves are quite simple in the light of what we know from revelation about God and the evil spirit.

FIRST PRINCIPLE: "God and the Angels, and the Devil, Act According to their Respective Natures"

Catholic theology defines God as infinitely good and powerful, all pure and holy, all wise and truthful. His angels share in these perfections according to their capacity, and never contradict them. But the devil is just the opposite. He is confirmed in wickedness and the personification of evil. He is the father of lies who uses all his intelligence to fight against God and everything holy. Accordingly when God acts upon the soul, His mode of operation will be characteristically different from that of the devil, and vice versa, so that each reveals his proper nature. Two of the rules of discernment are based upon this principle.

Divine Omnipotence Acting without a Preceding Cause: Since only infinite power can directly produce an effect without a proportionate natural cause, one index of divine activity on the soul is the presence of consolation "without any previous cause." For "it belongs solely to the Creator to come into a soul, to leave it, to act upon it, to draw it wholly to the love of His Divine Majesty."[1] Other rules need to be applied to recognize the source of consolation "preceded by a cause," e.g.,

[1] *Second Rules for the Discernment of Spirits,* Rule 2.

by previous reflection and prayer, which may be induced by the good or wicked spirit. But in the absence of antecedent causation, the agent must be God Himself exercising His sovereign power over the human spirit.

Reaction of Similar and Dissimilar Natures on Contact: Experience tells us that persons who are similar in character easily get along together, whereas opposite temperaments tend to clash and grate on each other. Hence the common description of compatible and incompatible personalities. The same holds true between human beings and the invisible characters of the spirit world.

Four combinations are possible: the human person may be good or bad, and in each case he may be acted upon either by the spirit of God or the powers of evil. In two cases, the combination is compatible and the consequent reaction agreeable. Thus "in souls that are progressing to greater perfection, the action of the good angel is delicate, gentle, delightful. It may be compared to a drop of water penetrating a sponge." And conversely, "in souls that are going from bad to worse," where "the disposition is similar to that of the (evil) spirits, they enter silently, as one coming into his own house when the doors are open." But where opposites meet, the reaction is entirely different. When a God-fearing man is assailed by the devil, "the action of the evil spirit is violent, noisy, and disturbing. It may be compared to a drop of water falling on a stone." Correspondingly when the good spirits are trying to shake a sinner out of his lethargy, "they enter with noise and commotion that are easily perceived" as alien to their nature.[2]

SECOND PRINCIPLE: "The Good and Evil Spirits Act for Contrary Purposes"

More than just acting according to their respective natures, the good and evil spirits operate on human souls for diametrically different ends. The good spirits, whether God directly or His angels and saints, are uniquely interested in guiding men

[2] *Ibid.*, num. 7.

to their eternal destiny in the beatific vision. All the light and inspiration they offer are intended to lead us closer to God. The devil and his minions intend the very opposite. Condemned to hell themselves, they envy our lot as adopted sons of God and heirs of heaven. In the permissive will of providence, they can incite us to sin and, if we allow them, cause our destruction by death in the enmity of God.

Consolations from the Good Spirit: Consistent with God's intention of leading us to Himself, one means He employs is to give us consolation in His service. According to St. Ignatius, "I call it consolation when an interior movement is aroused in the soul, by which it is inflamed with love for its Creator and Lord and, as a consequence, can love no creature on earth for its own sake, but only in the Creator of them all." Again "it is consolation when one sheds tears that move to the love of God," for whatever reason "that is immediately directed to the praise and service of God." And finally, consolation is "every increase of faith, hope, and love and all interior joy that invites and attracts to what is heavenly and to the salvation of one's soul by filling it with peace and quiet in its Creator and Lord."[3] God and His spirits, therefore, appeal to the fundamental instinct in human nature, which desires "joy, peace and quiet," first to wean us away from creatures and then invite and attract us to the love of heavenly things.

The Devil Induces or Capitalizes on Desolations: Among the obstacles which the devil places to impede our progress in virtue are the whole complex of negative sentiments which St. Ignatius calls by the general name of desolation, and which he describes as "darkness of soul, turmoil of spirit, inclination to what is low and earthly, restlessness rising from many disturbances, and temptations which lead to want of faith, hope and charity." The desolate soul is "wholly slothful, tepid, sad and separated, as it were, from its Creator and Lord."[4] This descrip-

---

[3] *First Rules*, num. 3.
[4] *Ibid.*, num. 4.

tion is meant to be inclusive and allows of varying degrees of duration and intensity.

It would be wrong to assume that the devil always directly intervenes to produce a state of desolation. Unless supported by divine grace, fallen human nature is quite capable by itself of depressing the spirit and dragging a soul down to the point of despair. But even where the devil may not be responsible for inducing desolation, he is always ready to exploit it for his own malicious ends. The devil, says Francis de Sales, uses unholy sadness as the breeding ground for all kinds of evil. "It disturbs the soul, disquiets her, arouses vain fears, disgusts her with prayer, overpowers the brain and makes it feeble, deprives the soul of wisdom, resolution, judgment and courage, and crushes her strength."[5] Ascetical writers consider this the most valuable weapon in the devil's armory, to make the service of God appear burdensome and discourage our perseverance in good.

With the same end in view, "it is characteristic of the evil one to fight against such happiness and consolation" as God and His angels may produce in the soul, "by proposing fallacious reasonings, subtleties, and continual deceptions."[6] Here we see the conflict of the Two Standards brought into the arena of the human heart, where the forces of evil are in open battle with the grace of God.

The Devil Tries to Hide his Evil Designs: Prominent among the devil's tactics are the efforts to conceal his evil intentions. Ignatius compares him to a false lover who tries to remain hidden and does not want to be discovered. The analogy is perhaps the strongest in the Exercises, but unmistakable. "If such a lover speaks with evil intention to the daughter of a good father, or to the wife of a good husband, and seeks to seduce them, he wants his words and solicitations kept secret. He is greatly displeased if his evil suggestions are revealed by the

---

[5] St. Francis de Sales, *Introduction to the Devout Life*, New York, 1923, p. 269.
[6] *Second Rules*, num. 1.

daughter to her father, or by the wife to her husband. Then he readily sees he will not succeed in what he has begun." In the same way, whenever the devil is tempting a soul, "he earnestly desires that his wiles and seductions be received and kept secret."[7]

As long as a person keeps the temptations to himself, the devil can easily overcome his resistance and lead him into sin. One reason is the close relation between dependence on the external structure of the Church and the dispensation of internal grace. If a man refuses to seek counsel from those who can assist him, he exposes himself to the dangers of illuminism, which derives from spiritual pride, and produces the excesses so familiar outside the true faith.

THIRD PRINCIPLE: "The Spirits Adapt Themselves to the Persons They Are Trying to Influence"

Something has already been seen of the way God and His angels, as well as the devil, adapt themselves to different persons in order to lead them to their respective ends. But St. Ignatius goes into considerable detail to analyze this principle of adaptation, especially on the part of Satan in regard to his prospective victims.

How the Good Spirit Adapts Himself to Good People and to Sinners: By good people, St. Ignatius understands "those who go on earnestly striving to cleanse their souls from sin and who seek to rise in the service of God to greater perfection." They are not necessarily living in the state of perfection and, on occasion, may fall into sin. But their habitual disposition is oriented towards obedience to God and a desire to keep in His friendship. With such people, the good spirit adapts himself accordingly, and seeks by every means to "give courage and strength, consolations, tears, inspirations, and peace. This he does by making everything easy, by removing all obstacles so that the soul may go forward in doing good."[8]

---

[7] *First Rules*, num. 13.
[8] *Ibid.*, nn. 1–2.

This is a law of divine Providence, that while proving His servants with all manner of trials, He always accompanies the cross with the gift of His peace, to make the trial bearable and internally sweet. Any other course of action would be unwise, not to say unjust, on the part of God. Christ declared that His yoke is sweet and His burden light; He told His followers not to be troubled or afraid, but always to be in peace. He promised, already in this life, a taste of heavenly beatitude to the poor in spirit, the pure of heart and to those who suffer persecution for justice's sake. If even in the natural order there is anticipated pleasure in the right use of the faculties of mind and sense, would this be contradicted in the order of grace, where the Holy Spirit of peace and joy dwells in the souls of the just, inviting them to use their supernatural powers according to the will of God?

In St. Ignatius' vocabulary, sinners are "those who go from one mortal sin to another," or simply "from bad to worse." With such persons, God and His angels act in a different way, by adapting themselves to the needs at hand. Where good people need to be encouraged in the practice of virtue by spiritual delectation, sinners must be discouraged from their evil habits by drastic shocks and warnings. "Making use of the light of reason," if faith has grown weak, the good spirit "will rouse the sting of conscience and fill them with remorse."[9]

Again the method agrees with all that we know of God's mercy toward sinners. Since His purpose is to make them realize their sad condition, He uses means that fit the situation. Worry and anxiety over their past life, suffering and pain created by their sins, fear of death and the punishments that follow, are graces of mercy calculated to stir the sinners' complacency and bring them back to God.

The Devil's Adaptation to Different Kinds of Persons: As might be expected, the devil acts at cross purposes. With those who are habitually in sin or not seriously intent on serving God, "he fills their imagination with sensual delights and grati-

⁹ *Ibid.*

fications, the more readily to keep them in their vices and increase the number of their sins."[10] Any other course of action would militate against his aim, to keep the sinner in his sin and oblivious of the voice of conscience.

But with good people, the demoniac strategy becomes more cunning and, in fact, so clever that most of the Rules of Discernment deal with this single issue. Allowing for minor differences, two kinds of good people are the object of devilish instigation: those moderately faithful in the practice of virtue, and those living in greater or less perfection. Satan's tactics are different for each class.

Without limiting this method to those of ordinary virtue, the devil normally attacks such people by creating difficulties in their service of God. He seeks to "harass them with anxiety, afflict them with sadness and raise obstacles backed by fallacious reasonings to disturb their souls. Thus he seeks to keep them from advancing."[11] More graphically, the devil acts like the commander of an army who explores the defenses of the enemy and attacks at the vulnerable point. He "investigates from every side all our virtues, theological, cardinal and moral. Where he finds the defenses of salvation weakest and most defective, there he attacks and tries to take us by storm."[12] In doing so, he invariably disquiets the soul that wants to be faithful to God, and by this sign can easily be recognized.

With persons more advanced in the way of perfection, the devil is more oblique. Where open attack would fail, he simulates the spiritual joys given by the good spirit in order to lead people astray. "He will pose as an angel of light and begins by suggesting thoughts that are suited to a devout soul, but ends by suggesting his own. . . . Afterwards he will endeavor little by little to finish by drawing the soul into his hidden snares and evil designs."[13]

Since the tactics are more shrewd, they are also more diffi-

10 *Ibid.*
11 *Ibid.*
12 *First Rules*, num. 14.
13 *Second Rules*, num. 4.

cult to discover. Hence the need of tracing the whole series of thoughts animated by the pseudo-consolation. When the devil uses the "open attack" method, his presence can be seen immediately in the disturbance he arouses in the soul. But when the method lies under cover of pious thoughts and consolations, it may take some time and examination before the devil is identified. According to St. Ignatius, when any course of thoughts suggested to us terminates in something evil or distracting, or less good than we had formerly done or proposed to do; when they end by weakening or disquieting the soul and destroy the peace and tranquillity it enjoyed before, no matter how holy or spiritual the thoughts may be, they should be suspect as coming from the devil.

One difficulty that bears some explanation is how to apply the Rules of Discernment when, as often happens, a person may be substantially faithful to the precepts of the Gospel but more or less careless in the spiritual life. How can he use the rules for consolation and desolation if he is not so bad as to be going "from mortal sin to mortal sin," nor so good as to feel he is "earnestly rooting out his sins and advancing daily from good to better"? Do the rules apply to him? Emphatically, yes. The general principles which govern the respective action of the good and evil spirits are the same, whether they operate on a person who is entirely good or bad, or on someone only mediocre and lax in virtue.

With due proportion, the spirits act in comparatively the same way towards tepid souls as they would towards those who are steeped in sin. The devil tries to inspire false security and deceptive peace of mind, while God and His angels seek to arouse the sluggard from tepidity. However, a subtle detail should be added. In order to use the rules effectively I must have at least some notion of my basic spiritual condition, how faithful I am to grace and in what areas I am negligent in the service of God. When a prospective course of action comes to mind (or has been undertaken) and it gives rise to anxiety and disquiet, I must inquire in what direction the anxiety is leading. Does it tend to inhibit or to assist what I know in conscience is the better part of me? If it hinders, the devil should be suspected; if it assists, the presence of God may be assumed. The same holds true when a sense of peace and tranquillity occurs. If this favors and makes easier the practice of things which reason and faith have always told me are God's will, the good spirit is most probably active; if it hinders this side of my moral life, the devil is most likely the agent.

Evidently the discernment becomes increasingly difficult if a person has been less faithful to the dictates of conscience and the inspirations of grace, because the fundamental norms for discernment (his ordinary spiritual attitude) are obscured. On the other hand, the greater his moral fidelity, the more easily will he detect the evil spirit as hindering his normal disposition to avoid sin at all costs and the more surely can he recognize the good spirit as encouraging his habitual intention to please God.

ASCETICAL ACTION FOLLOWING ON THE
DISCERNMENT

St. Ignatius was not content with giving a set of rules to distinguish good and evil spirits in their influence on the soul. He carried the discernment to its natural conclusion by offering a definite plan of action, or reaction, once the spirit is recognized.

How to Act in Consolation: Assuming that a spiritual consolation is known to be from God, to derive maximum profit from this visitation a man should first "consider how he will conduct himself during the time of desolation, and store up a supply of strength as defense against that day."[14] No doubt this storing of energy comes especially in the form of grace, to be prayed for in times of consolation; but it also means anticipating the future by thoughtful planning and fidelity to established habits, which are sure to be tested in the coming period of dryness and desolation.

[14] *First Rules*, num. 10.

Unless we are careful, in times of spiritual fervor we may be tempted to indulge in pride and presumption due to over-confidence. Consequently, "he who enjoys consolation should take care to humble himself . . . and recall how little he is able to do in times of desolation when he is left without [special] grace or consolation."[15] Otherwise, we run the risk of undertaking practices beyond our strength, or neglecting prudent safeguards of virtue that we thought was unassailable.

How to Act in Desolation: The basic rule to follow in times of spiritual depression is "never make any change, but remain firm and constant in the resolution and decision which guided us the day before the desolation, or in the decision to which we adhered in the preceding consolation."[16] Otherwise the whole benefit of the Exercises can be lost. To what purpose would a man raise himself to the third mode of humility and make the Election if a day or so later, under the spell of despondency, he went back on his decision? *Mutatis mutandis,* the same holds true for any resolution we make in the spiritual life—never to change it under the stress of desolation.

Instead of changing our mode of action, we should rather "intensify our activity against the desolation," by means of prayer, meditation, and additional penance. Equally profitable is reflection on the purpose that God has in permitting the devil to depress our ordinary fervor. He may want to remind us that "we have been tepid and slothful or negligent in our exercises of piety"; or may wish to try us "to see how much we are worth"; and certainly because "God wants to give us a true knowledge of ourselves," in order to make us more humble and better disposed to receive His graces and heavenly blessings.[17]

Just as sensible devotion tends to make us presumptuous and requires the corrective of humility, so desolation leads to discouragement and should be neutralized by whatever may strengthen our confidence in God. Under trial, we must "strive

15 *Ibid.*, num. 11.
16 *Ibid.*, num. 5.
17 *Ibid.*, num. 9.

to persevere in patience," and remind ourselves that "consolation will soon return." If we neglect to bolster our spirits in this way, we may give in to the demands of lower nature on the pretext that we have undertaken too much, and abandon certain practices in the spiritual life that we needed years to cultivate.

Courage in Resisting the Devil: As a cardinal principle in demonology, the devil is powerless against the grace of God. St. Ignatius compares him to a woman quarreling with a man. As long as he shows himself determined and fearless, she will give in and run away. "In the same way, the enemy becomes weak, loses courage and turns to flight with his seductions as soon as one leading a spiritual life faces his temptations boldly and does exactly the opposite of what he suggests."[18] But if we lose confidence in divine help and cringe before the devil's assault, "no wild animal on earth can be more fierce than the enemy of our human nature."

Manifesting the Devil's Intrigues: Since the devil wants to keep his machinations hidden, no single method of dealing with temptations is more valuable than to act against this urge to secretiveness. "If one manifests (these intrigues) to his confessor or to some other spiritual person who understands the devil's malicious designs, the evil one is very much vexed. For he knows that he cannot succeed in his evil undertaking, once his evident deceits have been revealed."[19] Sharing these internal experiences with a competent spiritual guide will require humility; but humility merits grace to recognize the devil's strategy and resist his instigations. It is also a mark of prudence to seek advice from accredited sources when the mind becomes troubled by vexatious thoughts, as happens in strong temptation; but again the proper use of our reason disposes the soul for divine assistance to overcome the enemy's designs.

[18] *Ibid.,* num. 12.
[19] *Ibid.,* num. 13.

13

Norms of Catholic Orthodoxy

A SUPERFICIAL reading of the Rules for Thinking with the Church may leave us with the impression that they are only a set of commonplace norms for living a Catholic life or a kind of dispensable addition to the Exercises. In reality they are a classic summation of the Ignatian spirit and so important that without them a retreat will be only partially effective in orientating a soul in its relations to God.

The best tradition on the origins of the rules says they were written either at Paris or in Italy, perhaps fifteen years after the retreat at Manresa where the Exercises were first begun. Scholars have partly traced the Rules to a list of seven questions which Francis I, King of France, ordered in 1535 to serve as the basis for conferences between theologians at the University of Paris and German Protestant divines. The latter were asked, e.g., "Whether they are willing to confess that the Church militant, founded by divine right, is unchangeable in faith and morals, and under our Lord Jesus Christ is headed by St. Peter and his successors down the centuries."[1] However, no single document did any more than suggest the rules as they stand in the book of the Exercises. Their real cause was the Protestant Reformation, from whose errors Ignatius wished to spare the faithful sons of the Church and inspire them with an intelligent zeal for the conversion of those who had lost the true faith. According to their author, the Rules of Orthodoxy

[1] Arturo Codina, *Los Origenes de Los Ejercicios Espirituales*, Barcelona, 1926, p. 204.

"should be observed to foster the true attitude of mind we ought to have in the Church Militant," which, the earliest commentators explain, refers to all types of retreatants, but especially two classes of persons: those who live and work among non-Catholics, and those engaged in the active apostolate. In modern times, this means practically everyone, priests, religious and the laity in every walk of life.

We gain some idea of the respect which these rules enjoy among Protestants from the latest edition of *Documents of the Christian Church* in the World's Classics, which cover all the main writings of Catholics and heretics during the centuries. Along with passages from the Council of Trent, the Rules of Orthodoxy are quoted in full to illustrate the spirit of the "Counter Reformation of the Roman Church."

I. THE CHURCH AND PRIVATE JUDGMENT

We must put aside all judgment of our own, and keep the mind ever ready and prompt to obey in all things the true Spouse of Christ our Lord, our holy Mother, the hierarchical Church.

In the first rule, St. Ignatius isolates the basic error of non-Catholic Christianity which claims that private judgment in doctrine and morals is according to the will of God. "You have been baptized and endowed with the true faith," Luther told his followers, "therefore you are spiritual and able to judge of all things by the word of the Gospel, and you are not to be judged by any man. Say, 'My faith is here a judge and may declare: This doctrine is true, but that is false and evil.' And the Pope and all his crew, nay, all men on earth must submit to that decision."[2] It was against this pretension to autonomy that Ignatius strove so zealously, because better than most of his contemporaries he foresaw what a brood of evils this spirit of independence would generate in the western world.

Where the original Reformers were satisfied with proclaiming man's freedom to interpret the Scriptures with no other

---

[2] Martin Luther, *Werke* (Weimar Ed.), Vol. XIII, p. 359.

guide than the Holy Spirit, their infidel disciples have since been emancipated even from a personal God. "If there were a God," writes Bertrand Russell, "I think it very unlikely He would have such an uneasy vanity as to be offended by those who doubt His existence."

As a sane alternative to this mad subjectivism, Ignatius offers the objectivity of the Catholic faith which cannot err because it is founded on the word of God. Assuming that his listeners are Catholic, he urges them to cultivate a disposition of soul which makes the will prompt and the mind prepared to obey whatever the Church prescribes. The will must acquire an instinctive desire to submit to the Church's authority and the mind should ever be ready to nourish the will with necessary motivation. Two motives are proposed: because the Church is the Spouse of Christ and because she is our Holy Mother.

Christ loves His Spouse in her members with a special predilection. For her sake He became man and died on the cross to save her; to her He committed the deposit of revelation, the sacramental system and the treasury of His graces. At Pentecost He sent her His own Spirit, through which He continues to animate the Church's body and sanctify her members. He has destined her to share in His heavenly kingdom for all eternity.

In return for this love of Christ, we who form the Church are to show our love for Him, as He said, by keeping His commandments. Our obedience to Him, therefore, should not be grounded on servile fear but on the deepest gratitude, and the greater demand this makes on our generosity, the better chance we have for proving our love for Him.

In keeping with patristic tradition, St. Ignatius appeals to the Church's motherhood as another motive for perfect obedience. As the Spouse of Christ, she gave us birth at baptism, which the Fathers have called the Church's womb. We are nourished on the food of her sacraments, protected by her laws and discipline, and instructed by her sacred doctrine. Our response should be a filial devotion, manifested by obedience to the Mother who gave us supernatural life and who desires our good even when her precepts place a burden on our love.

Furthermore, the character of our obedience to the Church is determined by her nature, which is hierarchical, and therefore implies subordination on a graduated level that even her enemies have praised for its efficiency. The remarkable thing, however, is not the Church's stratified authority but the fact that with God's grace this stratification has been kept intact for almost twenty centuries. What should this mean to me as a Catholic? It assures me that because I have a certain position in the Church's juridical structure; as layman or religious, priest or prelate, my obedience is not a vague submission to some undefined ecclesiocracy, but acceptance of the human agency placed above me as speaking with the voice of Christ. This requires no ordinary faith in God's providence, to recognize His will in the directives of another person like myself and perhaps inferior to me in many ways, except in the one mysterious way that he is vested with divine authority.

II. FREQUENT CONFESSION AND HOLY COMMUNION

We should praise sacramental confession, the yearly reception of the most Blessed Sacrament, and praise more highly monthly reception, and still more weekly Communion, provided requisite and proper dispositions are present.

If we assume that frequentation of the sacraments is a safe index of Catholic piety, this rule in the Exercises has contributed more than any other element in Ignatian spirituality to the upbuilding of the Church in modern times. The most authoritative witness for this judgment is Benedict XIV, who declared that "the universal Church owes especially to St. Ignatius and the Society founded by him the propagation of the practice of frequent confession and Holy Communion."[3]

By the middle of the sixteenth century, the sacraments were being received with notorious infrequency. In spite of the se-

[3] Benedict XIV, *De Servorum Dei Beatificatione et Beatorum Canonizatione,* Venice, 1767, Vol. III, p. 140.

vere threat of excommunication and deprivation of Christian burial passed by the Lateran Council in 1215, many Catholics did not make their Easter duty. At least one contemporary, St. Robert Bellarmine, felt this was the principal cause of the Protestant Revolt, that so many people stayed away from the sacraments. Consequently, "the unique and infallible way of reforming the Church of Christ would be to induce every Catholic to receive the Eucharist once a month or, better, once a week. With frequent Communion would come frequent confession, and with these two weapons there is no evil so inveterate it could not be overcome."[4] Bellarmine was only echoing the teaching of the Spiritual Exercises.

Present-day teaching on the frequency and dispositions for Holy Communion was crystallized in 1905 by the legislation of St. Pius X. His decree *Sacra Tridentina Synodus* settled many questions which had vexed theologians since the Middle Ages and thus inaugurated what Pius XII has called "the modern Eucharistic renascence."

1. In the very title of the decree, "On daily reception," he answered the question of what exactly frequent Communion means. Arguing from the analogy of food used by Christ Himself, and "the almost unanimous interpretation" of the Fathers that "daily bread" in the Lord's Prayer means daily Communion, Pius X concluded that "the Eucharistic Bread ought to be our daily food."[5]

2. But granted that daily Communion is permissible, is it commendable to all classes, priests and religious, lay people and children? Unequivocally, "the desire of Jesus Christ and the Church is that all the faithful should daily approach the sacred banquet."[6] This was directly contrary to the Jansenist rigorism which excluded most people from the holy table, "ex-

[4] St. Robert Bellarmine, *Opera Oratoria Postuma*, Rome, 1943, Vol. IV, p. 247.

[5] *Acta S. Sedis*, Vol. XXXIX, pp. 400–405. English translation by Ferreres, *The Decree on Daily Communion*, London, 1909, p. 25.

[6] *Ibid.*, p. 25.

cept once a week, or once a month, or once a year." Although implicit in the decree of 1905, frequent Communion for children had to be expressly promulgated in subsequent decrees: twice in 1906 to urge "frequent reception even for children," and in 1910 to require their admission to First Communion "as soon as they begin to have a certain use of reason."[7]

3. The vital question of necessary dispositions was answered by the Pope when he decided in favor of the minority school of theologians who required only the state of grace and a right intention. He explained that "a right intention consists in this: that he who approaches the holy table should do so, not out of routine or vainglory or human respect, but for the purpose of pleasing God, of being more closely united with Him by charity, and of seeking this divine remedy for his weaknesses and defects."[8] When it is remembered that moralists for centuries had required other conditions, such as absence of habitual venial sin, Pius X's decree stands out as a monument of generosity to the Catholic world.

4. Underlying the practical norms of the decree is a dogmatic principle which involves the nature and purpose of the Eucharist as a sacrament of the New Law. In the sixteenth century, the Reformers had so emphasized the remedial function of the Eucharist that the Council of Trent condemned "anyone who says that the principal fruit of the most Holy Eucharist is the remission of sins."[9] A century later and into modern times the Jansenists went to the other extreme. So far from considering the Eucharist remedial, they considered it only remunerative. The sub-title of the Jansenist classic on frequent Communion was *Sancta Sanctis*, meaning that no one but persons of high sanctity should receive the Eucharist, as a reward for their practice of virtue. St. Pius followed the Church's tradition in avoiding both extremes and at the same

[7] *Acta Apost. Sedis*, Vol. II, p. 580.
[8] Ferreres, *op. cit.*, p. 30.
[9] Denziger, 887.

time clarified the Catholic position on what the Protestants had exaggerated and the Jansenists practically denied, namely, that the Eucharist is an extension of the redemptive work of Christ. "The desire of Jesus Christ and the Church that all the faithful should daily approach the sacred banquet is directed chiefly to this end, that the faithful, being united to God by means of this sacrament, may thence derive strength to resist their sensual passions, to cleanse themselves from the stains of daily faults, and to avoid those graver sins to which human frailty is liable."[10]

Frequent confession in the sense of confessing only venial sins has been practised from earliest times. But like Holy Communion, the custom fell into abeyance until resuscitated by the Council of Trent. St. Ignatius was something of an innovator on this score, by urging weekly confession even for the laity and prescribing for priest members of his order confession *ad minimum* once a week.

The mind of the Church on frequent confession was authoritatively declared by Pope Pius XII in his encyclical on the Mystical Body, where he rebuked "the opinions of those who assert that little importance should be given to frequent confession of venial sins." He admits that venial faults can be remitted in other ways, but confessing them sacramentally we produce a variety of spiritual effects. "Genuine self-knowledge is increased, Christian humility grows, bad habits are corrected; spiritual neglect and tepidity are resisted, the conscience is purified, the will strengthened, a salutary self-control is attained and grace increased in virtue of the sacrament itself."[11] It should be noted that both in this encyclical and later when writing on the Sacred Liturgy, the pope branded as "completely foreign to the spirit of Christ and His Immaculate Spouse, and most dangerous to the spiritual life," any disparagement of frequent confession—which emphasizes the enduring value of St. Ignatius' regulation in the Spiritual Exercises.

[10] Ferreres, *op. cit.*, pp. 25–26.
[11] *Mystici Corpus*, p. 33.

III. LITURGICAL AND VOCAL PRAYER

We ought to praise the frequent hearing of Mass, the singing of hymns, psalmody, and long prayers whether in the church or outside; likewise the hours at fixed times for the whole Divine Office, for every kind of prayer, and for the canonical hours.

If ever the Spiritual Exercises are accused of being unliturgical, this rule gives the answer. Every phase of the liturgical life is encouraged by St. Ignatius, and should be so impressed upon the retreatants: the hearing of Mass, the recitation or chanting of the Divine Office, the singing of hymns, the offering of prayers at stated times and for specific ends. Ignatius' own devotion to the Holy Sacrifice was so great that he spent a full year in preparing to ascend the altar for the first time. "After his ordination," according to one who knew him intimately, "he hardly began to recite the canonical hours when he met with a serious difficulty. Spiritual consolation, interior feelings and tears flowed in upon him. It took him nearly a day to finish, and he wore himself out in the task. He could not be helped." Before the end of his life the trial became so heavy that the pope was asked to commute his recitation of the Office to a certain number of Paters and Aves. "But even so, the vehemence of his grace and the Spirit often threw him into an ecstasy."[12]

The original reason for recommending the liturgy in the Exercises was to neutralize the hatred of the sectarians for Catholic worship and external piety. Luther described the Mass as "a sacrilegious abuse," and the Office as "a confused sea of babbling and howling." Calvin denounced adoration of the Eucharist as idolatry, for which every popish priest deserved to be hanged. In our day, when the liturgical movement has developed to a degree unknown since the Reformation, the Ignatian attitude towards the liturgy has an ascetical value that may not be apparent. The public worship of God is not only rec-

[12] *Monumenta Historica*, "Scripta de S. Ignatio," Madrid, 1904, Vol. 1, p. 475.

ommended but considered essential to the spirit of Catholicism, and any de-emphasis of the liturgy savors of heresy. But, as Pius XII pointed out, the accent in the liturgical revival should be placed where it rightly belongs, within the minds and hearts of the faithful and not in external ceremonies. "The chief element of divine worship," he cautioned, "must be interior. For we must always live in Christ and give ourselves to Him completely, so that in Him, with Him, and through Him the heavenly Father may be duly glorified."[13]

Thus prudently balanced, the constant stress of the Exercises on personal holiness becomes perfectly, even necessarily, consonant with liturgical piety. Whether the liturgy is equated with Eucharistic worship, centered on the Mass and the Office in choir, or extended to every form of public devotion to God and the saints, the source of its efficacy, on man's side, remains the internal disposition with which the liturgy is performed. Even where grace is given *ex opere operato*, as in the sacraments, a certain minimal condition of soul must be present to make the sacraments fruitful, and their fruitfulness increases as the recipient is more detached from creatures and better disposed to do the will of God, which according to St. Ignatius is the whole purpose of the Spiritual Exercises.

IV–V. THE COUNSELS AND WORKS OF SUPEREROGATION

We must highly praise religious life, virginity, and continency; and matrimony ought not to be praised as much as any of these.

We should praise the vows of religion, obedience, poverty and chastity, and vows to perform other works of supererogation conducive to perfection. However, it must be remembered that a vow deals with matters that lead us closer to evangelical perfection. Hence, whatever tends to withdraw one from perfection may not be made the object of a vow, for example, a business career or the married state.

One of the surest signs of the heretical spirit against which

[13] *Mediator Dei*, p. 12.

Ignatius wrote the fourth and fifth rules is the denial of spiritual perfection as a lawful ambition of the Christian life. A contemporary statement of Protestant doctrine, the Anglican Articles of Religion, stated that "Voluntary works besides, over and above, God's commandments, which they call works of supererogation, cannot be taught without arrogance and impiety. For by them men do declare that they not only render unto God as much as they are bound to do, but that they do more for his sake, than of bounden duty is required: whereas Christ said plainly, 'When you have done all that is commanded to you, say, We are unprofitable servants.'"[14] This follows from the Protestant notion of man's nature as wholly corrupted by the fall and consequently incapable of contributing anything of its own even to rising from sinfulness, let alone performing acts of generosity beyond what is strictly mandatory.

If the Christian counsels and particularly virginity had to be vindicated in the sixteenth century, they must also be defended and promoted today. Although the excellence of virginity and celibacy, and their superiority over the married state were defined by the Council of Trent, "recent attacks on this traditional doctrine" prompted Pius XII to write an encyclical on the subject which might serve as a commentary on the two Rules we are considering.

1. It is against common sense, the faithful are told, to consider the sexual instinct as the most important and deepest of human desires, and to conclude from this that a person cannot restrain his passions for a life-time without injury to his nervous system or "the harmony of his personality."

2. Equally erroneous is the opinion that the sacrament of marriage, which gives grace *ex opere operato*, is a better instrument than virginity for uniting souls with God. If this were true, how could St. Paul recommend periodic abstinence as an aid to better prayer?

3. As a practical corollary to the preceding, those are to be

14 *The Book of Common Prayer*, New York, 1944, p. 605.

censured "who strive to turn young people away from the Seminary or Religious Orders and Institutes and from the taking of sacred vows, persuading them that they can, if joined in marriage, as fathers and mothers of families pursue a greater spiritual good by an open and public profession of the Christian life."[15]

There is a natural tie-up between these two rules and the retreat Election. Among the principal subjects for the Election is the choice of a state of life and its improvement, to be made with the fulness of generosity in imitation of Jesus Christ. If the retreatant has not yet made a choice, it is essential to a good retreat that he consider the life of virginity—in the priesthood, the religious life or the world—as a possible vocation to which God may be calling him. If the retreatant is a priest or religious (or destined to perpetual celibacy), the Election may take the form of remotivation to strengthen him against future temptations and develop his evangelical chastity. If he is in the married state, he should at least be urged to practice that self-restraint without which, as the national divorce rate is proving, men and women scarcely remain faithful to the obligations of their conjugal life.

VI–VIII. RELICS AND IMAGES, SAINTS AND INDULGENCES

We should show our esteem for the relics of the saints by venerating them and praying to the saints. We should praise visits to the Station Churches, pilgrimages, indulgences, jubilees, crusade indults, the lighting of candles in churches.

We ought to praise not only the building and adornment of churches, but also images and veneration of them according to the subject they represent.

The non-Catholic mind has not greatly changed since the time of St. Ignatius in its attitude towards the veneration of saints and the use of images and relics to foster piety. According to one highly-placed critic, "the veneration of images and

[15] Pius XII, Encyclical *Sacra Virginitas*, English translation, *American Ecclesiastical Review*, June, 1954, pp. 416–418.

the relics of saints is a practice which above most others is odious and absurd to the Protestant mind," which assumes that "images and relics are employed not as aids to devotion but as a channel, if not actually a fountain, of miraculous power."[16]

Catholic doctrine on the veneration of the saints, their relics and images, was solemnly defined by the Council of Trent. For our purpose, one statement of the Council has special bearing on the asceticism of the Spiritual Exercises. Among the reasons why saints should be venerated is the fact that through them "salutary examples are put before the eyes of the faithful, so that they fashion their lives and actions in imitation of the saints."[17] In other words, it is intrinsic to Catholic piety to strive after holiness not only by imitating Jesus Christ but also by following the saints whom the Church infallibly declares to have been the best imitators of their divine Master.

Spiritual heredity among the saints is a commonplace in Christian hagiography. When St. Paul told the Corinthians to be followers of him as he was of Christ, he intimated a principle that lies deep in the psychology of sanctity. Ignatius himself was converted by reflecting on the heroism of Saints Dominic and Francis of Assisi, and on more than one occasion in the Exercises he offers the virtues of the saints, especially the Blessed Virgin, for our imitation.

Our relation to the saints, therefore, is at least twofold: to beg their intercession for us before the throne of God, and to venerate them by imitating their imitation of Christ. Without suggesting which of the two functions, intercessory or exemplary, is more important, it seems the first has been taken for granted and the second frequently overlooked. Yet it is of capital importance as a guidepost on the road to sanctification. The saints were mere creatures like ourselves. Their virtues were perfections of a human spirit whose actions, even the

---

[16] Winfred E. Garrison, *A Protestant Manifesto*, New York, 1952, pp. 161–162.

[17] Denzinger, 987.

most heroic, were not essentially different than our own. They
drew their motive power and inspiration from the person of
Christ, giving us an example of how to follow His example and
proving by experience how sanctifying this imitation can be.
They lived in times and circumstances that reflect our own,
and suffered temptations not only from the devil and the
world, but also (except Mary) from the flesh and their fallen
nature. We see them as our companions in tribulation, whose
lives are at once a mirror of the sanctity of Christ and a picture
of our own peculiar trials. What we share in common with
them is a finite personality striving for perfection; what we ad-
mire and try to emulate is their transformation "through the
power and grace of Jesus Christ."

Not unlike the worship of saints, indulgences played a dominant role in the Protestant revolt, if only because most of
Luther's ninety-five theses of opposition to Rome dealt with
this subject. Perhaps in modern times indulgences do not enjoy the dogmatic reputation they had in the sixteenth century,
but they are still ascetically important and, in the spirit of the
Exercises, should not be overlooked. Preparing for confession,
the retreatant is told to examine what actions he may have
committed against "things approved by Superiors," notably
"indulgences, like those granted for confessions and Com-
munions offered to obtain peace." A judicious stress on the
gaining of indulgences will set in relief the profound difference
between Catholic and non-Catholic Christianity. When
Luther was condemned for teaching that "the treasures of the
Church, from which the Pope grants indulgences are not the
merits of Christ and the saints," the underlying error was not
regarding the character of indulgences but the nature of the
Catholic Church. The ultimate reason why the Church can
confer indulgences derives from her character as more than a
human society, however conceived, being the Mystical Body
of Christ which incorporates His own divine Spirit and of
which the Son of God is the Head.

VII. FASTING, ABSTINENCE AND EXTERIOR PENANCES

*We must praise the regulations of the Church with regard
to fast and abstinence, for example, in Lent, on Ember Days,
Vigils, Fridays and Saturdays. We should praise all works of
penance, not only those that are interior but also those that
are exterior.*

About the same year that St. Ignatius wrote the Rules of
Orthodoxy (1536), John Calvin published his *Institutes of the
Christian Religion*, where he decried "the superstitious observance of Lent which priests recommend as a holy imitation of
Christ, whereas it is plain that Christ did not fast in order to
set an example to others."[18] The general attitude of the Reformers is succinctly described by Melanchthon in the Confession of Augsburg, where he dismissed external penances as
"childish and useless activity."

The Catholic Church has never taught that Christ was a
penitent in His own right, expiating His own sins, which would
be blasphemy. But since apostolic times she has urged the
faithful to imitate Christ in salutary acceptance (and inflic-
tion) of pain, as a powerful instrument for moving the divine
mercy. Elsewhere in the Exercises, St. Ignatius gives three
reasons why external penances are chiefly used: first to satisfy
for past sins; secondly, in order to overcome oneself, i.e., subject the senses and all that is inferior to the superior forces of
the soul; and thirdly to obtain some special grace from God,
like a deeper sorrow for sin or the solution of a doubt or
difficult problem.

The satisfaction for past sins flows as a clear duty from the
dogmatic teaching of the Church that when a person sins
mortally he contracts two obligations before God: the stain of
culpability or guilt, for turning away from the Creator, and a
debt of eternal punishment, for turning instead to a creature.
When the sin is forgiven by salutary contrition, the stain of
guilt and eternal punishment are taken away, but temporal

[18] John Calvin, *Institutes of the Christian Religion*, Book 4, chap. 12,
num. 20.

punishment may still remain. Venial sins, too, may be forgiven without all the punishment they deserve being simultaneously removed. Hence the need for penance to remit the temporal penalty which remains, and which the practice of so many penitent saints leads us to believe may be considerable. "Since it is impossible for sin to go unpunished," says St. Augustine, "let it be punished by you lest it be punished by Him."[19]

Even non-Christians recognize the value of voluntary mortification to gain self-mastery and modern psychology confirms the Church's traditional doctrine. At least in the beginning, bodily mortification acts as a sort of depressor which tends to subdue by under-stimulation the more assertive emotions of the soul, something like dark hangings help to create an atmosphere of passivity and gloom. Frequent experiments indicate that a strong incentive for doing an unpleasant task is the reflection, "I have been able to do this before." Finally, a general readiness to bear suffering and pain can become habitual from the practice of mortification. By the repetition of penitential acts, the body and spirit can, within limits, become inured to the privation inherent in the faithful following of Christ, especially by a judicious emphasis on that type of mortification which best equips a person for meeting difficult situations in the future.

The utility of penance as a type of petition for grace rests on the teaching of Christ, who declared that some kinds of demon are not driven out except by prayer and mortification. Its doctrinal basis is a combination of two familiar Christian truths: that prayer is the ordinary method for obtaining divine grace, and that the merit of our actions largely depends on the degree of their voluntariety. Since prayer may be either explicit, as in formal petition, or implicit, as in every sacrifice, acts of mortification are implicit petitions for divine assistance addressed to the throne of God. Correspondingly, since attention and will energy are normally heightened in the more difficult actions of life, voluntary penance can increase the merit of

[19] St. Augustine, "Sermo 20," PL 38, 66.

ordinary prayer by making it more attentive and willful, and therefore adds to the efficacy of our prayer when joined to mortification.

IX. OBEDIENCE OF THE INTELLECT

We must praise all the commandments of the Church, and be on the alert to find reasons for defending but never for criticizing them.

It is not surprising that St. Ignatius should wish to transmit through the Exercises the same spirit of obedience to the Church that characterized the Constitutions of the religious order which he founded. What he wrote in the classic *Letter on Obedience*, that "whoever aims at making an entire and perfect oblation of himself, besides his will, must offer his understanding, which is the highest degree of obedience," applies with equal cogency outside the cloister and, in fact, comprehends the present rule.

There are three degrees of obedience, according to St. Ignatius. The first and lowest is the obedience of execution which carries a command into external effect, but without internal submission of the intellect and will. This, says Ignatius, scarcely merits the name of obedience. The second degree, or obedience of the will, is praiseworthy and highly meritorious because it involves the sacrifice of human freedom for the love of God. At the highest level stands obedience of the intellect which is possible because, except in the face of intrinsic evidence to the contrary, the will for its own motives can bend the understanding; it is reasonable because nothing could be more intelligent than submission of our minds to infinite wisdom; it is necessary to insure proper subordination in a hierarchical society and protect the subject from internal conflict; and it is perfect because it immolates our noblest faculty and thereby renders the greatest glory to the divine majesty.

Retreatants generally need to be told that the degrees of perfection in evangelical obedience are equally valid in the ecclesiastical obedience for the Rules of Orthodoxy. Just as a religious in obedience to his institute can be satisfied with external observance, or can rise to conformity of his will and intellect with the Superior, so a Catholic of whatever rank may adopt the same three attitudes regarding the commandments of the Church. And if he rises to the degree of intellectual submission, his obedience has reached its highest perfection, within the ambit of divine precept as distinct from the evangelical counsels.

When St. Ignatius urges obedience to the precepts of the Church, he recommends this third degree, which requires a conformity of the whole man with the dictates of authority: of his body for external execution, his will for internal submission and his mind for perfect consent. The function of the mind "is to find reasons to defend" the Church's commandments against an unruly tendency to disobedience partly occasioned by the nature of the Christian religion, and partly determined by the character of the precept and the attitude of the person affected.

Sometimes we overlook the fact that Christianity is founded on the truths of revelation which demand our belief in the word of God. This holds quite as much for truths that are naturally knowable as for strict mysteries, and as much for doctrines that are simply to be believed as for commandments that are also to be obeyed. Since, therefore, faith is essentially obscure, i.e., accepted on divine authority and not because intrinsically evident, its very nature places a burden on the intellect that needs to be recognized and properly handled. For example, the Church tells me to assist at Mass on Sunday under penalty of mortal sin. The human mind, no matter how intelligent, will never see on purely rational grounds why the Sunday precept should be so grave or even why hearing Mass is important. Apart from revelation, a man has no motive for going to Mass on Sunday and he will naturally rebel against the imposition unless he has faith and acts on the reasons that faith proposes for submitting to the obligation. The fundamental reason is the Church's divine mission, given to her by

Christ, to establish laws and prescribe their observance under pain of sin. Corollary motives are the dignity of the Mass and the necessity of grace, with all their implications. These and similar reasons must be accepted on faith, and, when need arises, invoked in order to obey the Sunday precept intelligently. The same applies to all the commandments of the Church, and not only the universal precepts but every command, even personal, made by valid ecclesiastical authority.

There is another aspect to the obedience of the intellect. Besides the essential need for finding reasons to defend the Church's commandments, as explained, other needs may also arise. It may happen that a command seems unreasonable on the score of inefficiency, ineptitude, or any one of a dozen natural causes. Assuming that due representation has been made and there is no suspicion of sin if the order is carried out, the obedient man in the Ignatian sense will look for reasons to support the precept or regulation and instinctively avoid any mental criticism. The ground for this attitude is again a matter of faith. From a natural standpoint the order may be a poor decision and scarcely suited to achieve the purpose intended, but supernaturally I know that my obedience can never be fruitless. When the apostles cast their nets into the water at the bidding of Christ, they were obedient, as Peter said, only to the word of the Master; and the miraculous draught which followed symbolizes this higher than ordinary providence, which disposes all things surely to their appointed end as foreseen and directed by God and beyond the calculations of men. There is no question here of conceiving a *deus ex machina* or relying on miracles, while admitting their possibility. It is rather a firm belief that my submission to the divine will has a guarantee of success that I can always hope for from the One whom I ultimately obey, because it involves the prevision of a myriad hidden forces, which He infallibly foresees, and their infinite combinations, which He infallibly designs.

Or again, the difficulty with obeying ecclesiastical authority may be a persuasion that the commandment is too hard for me. Marital obligations interpreted by the Church are examples of this difficulty. To meet it effectively over a period of years and in spite of a hostile atmosphere requires courage of a high order, which in turn requires cultivation of the mental attitude prescribed in the Rules of Orthodoxy. Feelings of inadequacy, poor health, the memory of past failures, the dread of being estranged or humiliated, and the fear of all sorts of possibilities, real or imaginary, will conspire to make a precept of obedience seem like a piece of tyranny unless the mind uses a heavy counterpoise to maintain a balanced judgment. The counterpoise, which comes from the deposit of faith, is a settled conviction that "God does not command the impossible. But when He commands, He warns you to do what you can, and also to pray for what you cannot do, and He helps you so that you can do it. For His commandments are not burdensome; His yoke is easy and His burden light."[20] This conviction is indispensable. Unless nourished and developed, even the gravest obligations of the Catholic religion will be disobeyed and their gravity obscured by the pressure of the emotions on the mind. Moreover, as Ignatius recommends, we should do more than defend the Church's laws against the objections of our lower nature, we must avoid criticizing them, not only to others but especially to ourselves. Psychologically this can be a talisman for protecting our obedience and raising it to a high degree of excellence. As objections arise, the will stands on the alert to order the mind to reject them, not dally with them and above all not to put them into action. In order to do this rationally, the will must be properly motivated and can draw its motives from the whole gamut of reason and revelation. Peace of mind, personal integrity, an effective apostolate, trust in God—in fact, anything which answers the need of the moment —can be used. The important thing is to use it and to know that human nature is so vacillating that any mood or stream of

[20] Denzinger, 568.

thought, no matter how oppressive, will pass away if it is not encouraged but resisted to the best of our ability.

X. RESPECT FOR OBEDIENCE UNDER TRIAL

We should be more ready to approve and praise the orders, recommendations, and way of acting of our superiors than to find fault with them. Though some of the orders, etc., may not have been praiseworthy, yet to speak against them, either when preaching in public or in speaking before the people, would rather be the cause of murmuring and scandal than of profit. As a consequence, the people would become angry with their superiors, whether secular or spiritual. But while it does harm in the absence of our superiors to speak evil of them before the people, it may be profitable to discuss their bad conduct with those who can apply a remedy.

"This was the special gift of God to St. Ignatius," according to Pius XI, "to lead men back to the practice of the virtue of obedience."[21] The order which he founded was to be so dedicated to this virtue that a special vow of obedience to the pope was to be added to the three substantial ones of evangelical perfection. All through life, in formal directives and in letters of spiritual counsel, it was obedience that Ignatius emphasized. In this respect the Exercises are no exception, starting from the examination of conscience before the general confession and ending with the Rules for Thinking with the Church.

The striking feature of the rule we are considering is not its insistence on the value of obedience, which may be assumed, but that it boldly deals with the delicate question of how to act when superiors or their directives are apparently out of order. No other passage in the Exercises was more carefully weighed and qualified than the present rule which, in the author's opinion, is one of the most realistic statements of St. Ignatius.

All kinds of superiors are included, "temporal as well as spiritual"; consequently everyone who has authority in the

[21] Pius XI, Apostolic Letter on the third centenary of the canonization of St. Ignatius, *Acta Apost. Sedis*, Vol. XIV, p. 628.

Church or civil society, from the pope or head of the national government to the lowest constabulary members. Also every possible source of criticism is visualized. It may be a law or regulation, a recommendation or simple counsel, the personal habits or conduct of an official or superior, either at present or in the past. Regardless of the source or the person concerned, the guiding principle should be a readiness to approve and praise rather than blame, and this will determine the course to be followed when anything censurable is found in those in authority.

Superiors are not to be criticized in public, whether in formal discourse or conversation with ordinary people, because this will give rise to scandal and complaints, without correcting the evil criticized. Common experience proves this fact, of which the Protestant Revolt is a tragic example. Thousands of simple people who had no special grievance against the pope and the bishops were whipped to a frenzy of hatred for the Church's authority by the fulmination of the Reformers. No matter how valid the complaint may be, there is no wisdom in exposing the evil before an emotional public which, at least in the Church's juridical structure, cannot apply an effective cure. If anything, the correction may be delayed or prevented altogether after men's feelings are aroused and demands are made for radical changes dictated by passion instead of prudence and considerate reason.

Right judgment suggests and circumstances may even oblige the exposure of maladministration or defects of character in persons of authority. But if the end in view is to correct an objective evil, the criticism will not be made indiscriminately, but only to those who can effect a suitable remedy. When civil authorities in a democratic society are concerned, this may require public censure before the people, but even then within the limits of justice and right order, with the intention to promote a common good and not simply to make news or discredit a hostile political party.

This "readiness to approve" the dictates and person of authority is the keystone of the Church's social stability. It anticipates two factors that are inseparable from any human society, not excluding the Mystical Body on its human side. Where men are in authority there will be weakness and mistakes, from which Christ did not fully exempt His Church except on the highest level, where the universal interests of salvation are concerned. Unless the faithful had this antecedent readiness to approve the policy and conduct of their ecclesiastical superiors, the natural tendency to criticism and independent judgment would dominate, and obedience would become difficult if not impossible. Finally, an element seldom considered in church and state discussions is the contribution which the true Catholic spirit makes to the peace and prosperity of civil society. It teaches the faithful to praise the laws of the state and the person of secular rulers, and abstain from any criticism, however provoked, that destroys the respect for public authority. So intrinsic to her doctrine is the Church's belief that "all authority is from God," that this fact alone should commend her to the state as a most faithful ally, whose allegiance is a matter of principle accepted on the word of God.

XI. POSITIVE AND SCHOLASTIC THEOLOGY

We should praise both positive theology and that of the Scholastics.

It is characteristic of the positive doctors, such as St. Augustine, St. Jerome, St. Gregory, and others, to rouse the affections so that we are moved to love and serve God our Lord in all things.

On the other hand, it is more characteristic of the scholastic doctors, such as St. Thomas, St. Bonaventure, the Master of the Sentences, and others, to define and state clearly, according to the needs of our times, the doctrines that are necessary for eternal salvation, and that help to refute and expose more efficaciously all errors and fallacies.

Further, just because scholastic doctors belong to more recent times, they not only have the advantage of correct understanding of Holy Scripture and of the teaching of the saints
and positive doctors, but, enlightened by the grace of God,
they also make use of the decisions of the Councils and of the
definitions and decrees of our holy Mother Church.

Any question why the Exercises should include a rule on
theological method is answered by a glance at the history of
the Reformation. In order to be freed from the Church's authority, the Reformers discarded the teachings of tradition and
canonized the Bible as the only norm of faith. Their bibliolatry led them to discredit first the Fathers of the Church and
then her scholastic Doctors, whose unanimous testimony to
the Roman Primacy was a refutation of Protestant autonomy.
When Luther brazenly declared that "Jerome should not be
numbered among the teachers of the Church because he was
a heretic," or "St. Augustine and St. Ambrose cannot be compared with me," he was perfectly in character.[22] Yet if it suited
his fancy, he appealed to patristic authority against the teachings of the Church, as when he rejected part of the Old Testament on the strength of a private opinion of St. Jerome. But
there was no compromise with scholastic teachers like Thomas
Aquinas, whose clear explanation of Catholic doctrine was a
constant irritant to the Reformers.

However, the present Rule of Orthodoxy has more than historical interest. Its accent on scholastic theology expresses a
permanent need for preserving the Church's dogmatic integrity against heretical opposition and, no less, against the tendency to uncontrolled speculation among her own members.
At the turn of the century, St. Pius X condemned as "Modernists, those who exalt positive theology in such a way as to
despise the scholastic."[23] And more recently, Pius XII complained that some Catholic lovers of novelty "easily pass from

[22] Martin Luther, *Table Talk*, New York, 1952, p. 261.
[23] St. Pius X, Encyclical *Pascendi*, English translation, London, 1937, p. 59.

disdain of scholastic theology to neglect or even despise the Magisterium of the Church."[24]

The relevance of this attitude to priest and seminary retreat-ants need scarcely be elaborated. Through the Exercises they can be helped to arrive at a balanced appreciation of both posi-tive and scholastic theology. If the second is exaggerated at the expense of the first, priests and teachers may be able to refute heretics and know the theological value of a thesis but not be ready "to stir up the affections to the love and service of God," which is indispensable in the ministry. On the other hand, and with Ignatian emphasis, if positive theology overshadows the scholastic, those who are to guide and instruct others will not have the scientific hold on revelation required "to explain for our times what is necessary for salvation, and to expose all er-rors and fallacies." Whatever need there was for scholastic theology in Ignatius' day, it is greater than ever today when the educational level of the faithful (and of the world in which they live) has reached an all-time high, and consequently calls for a deep and intelligent grasp of the faith.

XII. PRUDENCE IN EVALUATING SANCTITY

We must be on our guard against making comparisons be-tween those who are still living and the saints who have gone before us. For no small error is committed if we say, "This man is wiser than St. Augustine. He is another St. Francis or even greater. He is equal to St. Paul in goodness and sanctity."

The historical occasion for this rule seems to have been the number of false mystics and dubious saints that plagued the Church in the sixteenth century, so that Ignatius himself was imprisoned for a while on suspicion of being one of the *alum-brados*. The danger against which he cautions is deception due to hasty judgment in favor of a living person's sanctity or re-puted mystical experiences. If there is less of a problem today, it is only a matter of degree. A recent statement of the Assessor

[24] Pius XII, Encyclical *Humani Generis*, English translation, Weston, Mass., 1951, p. 19.

of the Holy Office warns against the current wave of pseudo-revelations in Catholic circles and cautions priests especially about the danger to souls unless their natural credulity is properly restrained.[25]

As a general norm which underlies St. Ignatius' rule, we should regularly prefer the virtue of canonized saints to that of living persons, no matter how great their reputation for sanctity. Unless they were martyrs, saints would not have been canonized unless they had practiced heroic virtue. And, in fact, one of the main reasons why they are raised to the honors of the altar is precisely to serve as models for our imitation. The long years of scrutiny into their writings and conduct, plus the Church's assistance from the Holy Spirit, give us an assurance of holiness that no living person can duplicate with equal certainty. Not the least benefit of a retreat, therefore, is to acquire a better appreciation of spiritual reading, with concentration on the lives and writings of the saints.

Therefore the normal attitude to adopt towards contemporary revelations and mystical phenomena should be one of great reserve. Within less than a decade, the hierarchy of at least six countries (Italy, France, Belgium, Germany, the Philippines and the United States) had publicly to censure the unauthorized popular approval of reported supernatural communications. In spite of the canonical prohibition against "books and pamphlets which treat of new apparitions, revelations, visions, prophecies and miracles" (Canon 1399), there is no lack of such publications readily available to Catholics, who need to be reminded of the Church's legislation and impressed with the harm that a single brochure of this kind can cause. On the practical side, in line with spiritual reading, the writings of genuine mystics like Teresa of Avila and John of the Cross, and accounts of authentic revelations and miracles like Lourdes and Fatima, should be recommended. Very often people indulge in useless or harmful reading in this area be-

[25] Card. Alfredo Ottaviani, *Osservatore Romano*, February 4, 1951.

cause they have not been introduced to the treasury of mysticism which the Church has approved and which offers one of her main titles to sanctity.

XIII. PERFECT SUBMISSION TO THE CHURCH'S MAGISTERIUM

If we wish to proceed securely in all things, we must hold fast to the following principle: What seems to me white, I will believe black if the hierarchical Church so defines. For I must be convinced that in Christ our Lord, the bridegroom, and in His spouse the Church, only one Spirit holds sway, which governs and rules for the salvation of souls. For it is by the same Spirit and Lord who gave the Ten Commandments that our holy Mother Church is ruled and governed.

Probably no statement of the Exercises has been more quoted and criticized by non-Catholics than St. Ignatius' directive that "What seems to me white, I will believe black if the hierarchical Church so defines it." Even Catholics may suspect something strange in being asked to contradict their convictions. Yet there are few mental attitudes that need to be more urgently cultivated than the willingness to submit our private judgment to the infallible teaching of the Church.

The difficulty arises from a misconception of the nature of faith, which is an intellectual assent to revealed truth, made with the assistance of supernatural grace and under the influence of the will; as against the Protestant Reformers who claimed that faith was an act of the will, wherein I trust that God's mercy has covered over, without actually deleting, my past sins. For if faith is essentially volitional, conformity of mind with objective truth is dispensable, and even in its absence I may be said to believe as long as I vaguely trust in the goodness of a God about whose nature and relations to me I may be in doubt. There can be no white or black, i.e., true or false, under this notion of faith, and the variety of sectarian opinions on such fundamentals as the Trinity and Incarnation followed logically on the denial of the intellectuality of faith and reducing it to an operation of the will or the blind instinct of religious feeling.

However, the present rule also pertains to Catholics who consider faith an act of the mind, on which the edifice of all the other virtues depends. While knowing this and perhaps because of this knowledge, they may not appreciate the function of the will in placing an act of faith and consequently fail to use this power as they ought, especially when some teaching of the Church seems to contradict their own judgment. For the laity, a truth like the sinfulness of divorce with remarriage is a good example. Married people can be so involved under various emotional pressures as to convince themselves that divorce and "trying again" are perfectly all right. Then arises a familiar clash of judgments, personal and ecclesiastical. To me divorce may seem white, but the Church says it is black, so I submit my intellect. But is this possible? Yes, for two reasons. First, because in the instance divorce *seems* to me to be white and therefore I do not know it is white with the same assurance that I exist or that two and two are equal to four. Secondly and more pertinently, since faith means the acceptance of God's word that something is true, my will can command the intellect to believe—indeed it must—without any violence to my rationality. In secular affairs most of our daily actions are directed by this kind of creedal knowledge, where the free will orders the mind to believe, on the word of other people who are just as fallible as myself. "If we receive the testimony of men," says St. John, "the testimony of God is greater," and therefore to be followed, my own judgment to the contrary notwithstanding.

But granted that my will should command the intellect to believe, how can I do this when, in a crisis, all my emotions are against some doctrinal position of the Church? The method is not despotic but diplomatic, and demands conscious remotivation of the will by concentrating attention on a great benefit to be gained or a terrible evil avoided in order to have the imperative faculty command a reluctant intellect to assent.

Quietly but deliberately I recall the advantages of submitting
to the Church's magisterial authority—peace of mind, the consolation of receiving the sacraments, the promise of special assistance from God, the security of my salvation; likewise the
harm that will follow if I do not believe—the torment of conscience, deprivation of sacramental graces, loss of merit and the
friendship of God and the risk of losing my soul. Braced by the
supernatural help which is never wanting, my will becomes
disposed to enjoin the mind to believe, moved ultimately by
the conviction that the same Spirit which governs the world
and its destiny also animates the Catholic Church and her
teaching, but proximately urged by the hope of reward or the
dread of God's punishment for belief or unbelief.

It may help us appreciate the power of the will to move the
intellect by seeing what happens whenever a person falls into
error. In the face of all evidence to the contrary, he can declare
that something is true or false simply because he wants it to be
so. He may refuse to examine the evidence offered, or, having
the evidence, will not see it through the haze of emotion or
prejudice which the will does not care to remove. A large part
of modern advertising is based on this principle: that properly
stimulated the most irrational impulses can be activated and
the mind made to believe that an article is necessary or useful,
not on the score of objective need but by the force of suggestion operating on the credulous will. The moral is obvious. If
the will can so easily sway the mind in the direction of error,
in the absence of objective evidence, why not in the direction
of truth, when the latter has only to be looked at willfully to
be recognized?

XIV–XV. SOME CAUTIONS ON PREDESTINATION

*Granted it is very true that no one can be saved without
being predestined and without having faith and grace, still we
must be very cautious about the way in which we speak of all
these things and discuss them with others.*

We should not make a habit of speaking much about pre-

destination. If somehow at times it comes to be spoken of, it must be done in such a way that the people are not led into any error. They are at times misled, so that they say: "Whether I shall be saved or lost, has already been determined, and this cannot be changed whether my actions are good or bad." So they become indolent and neglect the works that are conducive to the salvation and spiritual progress of their souls.

When St. Ignatius warned against careless preaching on the subject of predestination, he had more in mind than protecting the faithful from needless worry about their future destiny. In the *Institutes of the Christian Religion*, John Calvin laid down a principle which, carried to its logical extreme, would subvert not only Christianity but the foundation of all religion. "By predestination," wrote Calvin, "we mean the eternal decree of God, by which He has decided in His own mind what He wishes to happen in the case of each individual. For all men are not created on an equal footing, but for some eternal life is pre-ordained, for others eternal damnation."[26]

Always practical, Ignatius recognized predestination as a deep mystery which must be handled carefully in preaching and public discussion because, unlike other doctrines, it is too intimately bound up with human responsibility to be treated only academically. Even appealing to the Fathers may be risky. To quote St. Augustine, for example, that "the great majority of mankind is not saved,"[27] would hardly be encouraging.

St. Francis de Sales confessed that one of the heaviest trials of his life was the obsessing fear he had as a young man that he was certainly damned. It came upon him as the result of careless teaching on the subject of predestination. "If I am not fortunate enough to belong to those who are predestined," he said to himself, "I should never succeed in sanctifying myself and consequently lose the love of God for all eternity." After months of a violent struggle he finally shook off the temptation, once he realized that predestination is not independent

---

[26] *Institutes*, Book 3, chap. 21.
[27] St. Augustine, "Enchiridion," PL 40, 276.

of our use of God's grace, and therefore not an arbitrary commitment to heaven or to hell.

Although, as a general rule, "we should not make a habit of speaking much about predestination," this allows plenty of latitude. Perhaps there is less danger of discussing the subject nowadays than there was in the sixteenth century, when Calvinism was in the air, or in the 1700's, when Jansenism infected whole schools of theology. But whenever discussing predestination, the treatment must be dogmatically sound and properly balanced, so that man's autonomy is not absorbed by the divine sovereignty. Otherwise, as Ignatius warns, men will neglect the works that lead to salvation because, they say, God has already determined whether I shall be saved or lost; consequently it makes no difference what I do.

Historians trace the beginnings of rationalism to the Reformation doctrine of absolute predestination, as illustrated in men like Thomas Jefferson, who repudiated Christianity on the score that "it would be more pardonable to believe in no God at all, than to blaspheme Him by the atrocious attributes of Calvin."[28] Modern Catholics, especially intellectuals, are in too frequent contact with both streams of thought, Protestantism and infidelity, not to require light and protection in handling (without solving) one of the deepest problems of human existence.

XVI. FAITH AND GOOD WORKS

In the same way, great caution is necessary lest by much talk about faith, and much insistence on it without distinction or explanation, occasion be given to the people, whether before or after they have faith informed by charity, to become slothful and lazy in good works.

The Spiritual Exercises have been described as a Catholic reaction to the Protestant theory of faith without good works.

---

[28] Adrienne Koch and William Peden, *The Life and Selected Writings of Thomas Jefferson*, New York, 1944, pp. 705–706.

While over-simplified, the estimate is correct in highlighting the fundamental thesis of Ignatian spirituality, which is the service of God, as against the sectarian isolation of trustful confidence or faith as the essence of the Christian life. Luther's caricature of the two positions is worth quoting in full:

A Capuchin says, 'Wear a grey coat and a hood, a rope around the body and sandals on your feet.' A friar says, 'Put on a black hood.' An ordinary papist says, 'Do this or that work, hear Mass, pray, fast, and give alms.' But the true Christian says, 'I am justified and saved only by faith in Christ, without any works or merits of my own.' Compare these together and judge which is the true righteousness.[29]

This confidence in God without works of my own is not a historical relic that has only speculative value for professional theologians. It has entered modern thought at so many angles that Catholics should at least be alert to recognize its presence, no matter how disguised.

More directly, however, those who teach sacred doctrine are warned against speaking so much about faith, without qualification, that they obfuscate the rest of Catholicism. The question here is quite distinct from the erroneous concept of faith as opposed to good works, excogitated by the Reformers. Even the true notion of faith as assent to God's revelation should not be stressed to the point of obscuring other equally grave duties of the Christian life. We would never subscribe on principle to the thesis that no matter what a man does in the moral order, if he has the true faith he should not be overly blamed because a believing Catholic, though bad, is better than a law-abiding pagan. There are no grounds for the accusation that professing the Catholic creed absolves a man from other responsibilities; confession and indulgences will take care of whatever guilt was incurred. Nevertheless there are times when the bad example of nominal Catholics may not be sufficiently criticized, or the danger of scandal so minimized that people

[29] *Table Talk*, p. 190.

outside the Church draw the mistaken conclusion that we subordinate ethical values to doctrinal conformity.

XVII. GRACE AND FREE WILL

Likewise we ought not speak of grace at such length and with such emphasis that the poison of doing away with liberty is engendered.

Hence, as far as possible with the help of God, one may speak of faith and grace that the Divine Majesty may be praised. But let it not be done in such a way, above all not in times which are as dangerous as ours, that works and free will suffer harm, or that they are considered of no value.

The radical error of the Reformation was to make the grace of God the only operative agent in the performance of good works. "I will not lie or dissemble before God," wrote Luther, "I am not able to effect the good which I intend, but await the happy hour when God shall be pleased to meet me with His grace."[30] This was correlative to saying that "after the fall of our first parents, we have altogether a confounded, corrupt, and poisoned nature, both in body and soul; throughout the whole of man there is nothing that is good. Free will is utterly lost."[31]

When St. Ignatius called "poisonous" the "teaching which takes away free will," he allowed himself this rare epithet because he saw latent here the seed of a blind determinism that could, as it did, vitiate the moral principles of a large segment of the western world. Ostensibly pious because it seemed to give due credit to God for our practice of virtue, the doctrine of *sola gratia* actually made God a monster of iniquity by making Him responsible for our sins and reduced man to less than a manikin by denying him the faculty of choice in his service of God.

It is no coincidence that when Jansenism arose in the seventeenth century, St. Vincent de Paul declared "the new heresy

[30] *Ibid.*, p. 160.
[31] *Ibid.*, p. 165.

All My Liberty

can best be understood if Jansenius is viewed as the antithesis of St. Ignatius." Among other points of contradiction with the author of the Spiritual Exercises, Jansenius held that "in the state of fallen nature, interior grace is never resisted." We have no intrinsic power of resistance. Consequently, "to merit or demerit in the state of fallen nature, man does not need to have freedom from (internal) necessity, but freedom from (external) constraint is enough."[32] Again there is the same preoccupation with God's absolute sovereignty as in Luther and Calvin, with the same disastrous potential against which Ignatius had warred a hundred years before. By depriving man of responsibility for his moral actions, Jansenism paved the way for the French Revolution and the "Age of Reason," whose infidelity spread far beyond the confines of France and encouraged, among others, the deistic philosophy of England and colonial America.

The plain lesson which the present rule intends to teach is prudence in speaking of supernatural grace and not allowing a laudable desire of extolling the Divine Majesty to hide the elusive power of human freedom. We are here in the presence of a mystery, perhaps the deepest and certainly the most consequential in moral conduct. However there is something tantalizing about mysteries that should keep the teacher or preacher always on his guard. Faced with a mystery, we are tempted to resolve the problem by cutting the Gordian knot and accepting a rational explanation which satisfies the mind at whatever cost. In the mystery of man's cooperation with divine grace the "rational" alternatives are comparatively easy: either say that God so completely rules His creatures that despite appearances to the contrary, we are not free agents in the work of salvation but everything we do is entirely produced by Him. Or say that man is so fully master of his destiny that he is independent of God in the practice of virtue and, if anything, freely determines the Creator to give him what he needs. Both solutions are heretical, the first Protestant and the

[32] Denzinger, 1093–1094.

second Pelagian, and both are seductive to the natural man.
Both errors are still prevalent in modern times, with perhaps a
stronger temptation among believing Christians to ignore their
native liberty in favor of divine omnipotence, which points up
the need for greater caution against this kind of aberration, as
indicated by St. Ignatius.

XVIII. THE FEAR AND LOVE OF GOD

*Although the zealous service of God our Lord out of pure
love should be esteemed above all, we ought also to praise
highly the fear of the Divine Majesty. For not only filial fear
but also servile fear is pious and very holy. When nothing
higher or more useful is attained, it is very helpful for rising
from mortal sin, and once this is accomplished, one may easily
advance to filial fear, which is wholly pleasing and agreeable to
God our Lord since it is inseparably associated with the love
of Him.*

St. Ignatius was concerned to preserve the value of fear
against the Protestant hostility to this virtue as a valid motive
in the spiritual life. Among the doctrines on justification defined by the Council of Trent is a condemnation of anyone
who says that "the fear of hell, which makes us turn to the
mercy of God in sorrow for sins or which makes us avoid sin,
is itself sinful or makes sinners worse than they were before."[33]

The specific object of the last Rule of Orthodoxy is to urge
the importance of a salutary fear of God as a means of avoiding
grievous sin. To appreciate fully the wisdom of this recommendation, we must review the different kinds of fear that theologians, following St. Thomas and the teachings of Trent, have
distinguished with relation to sin.

On the broadest level, there is a fear of creatures that may
lead a person to offend God and that, in some form or another,
enters into the previous motivation of almost every sin. Thus
from fear of losing his reputation a man tells a lie, or out of
dread of persecution a Catholic denies his faith. St. Thomas

[33] *Ibid.*, 818.

calls this worldly fear. At the other extreme is a fear of the Creator which can move us to sacrifice a creature that would otherwise lead us to sin. Every meditation of the retreat presupposes this type of fear, which Ignatius commended in the final paragraph of the Spiritual Exercises.

But not every fear of God is necessarily good. If it is a slavish dread that cringes only at God's punishments and does not detach the heart from sin; if I remain attached to sinful intentions but, out of fear of being punished, fail to carry them into overt effect—there is no merit in my conduct and no profit, except the possible restraint which keeps me from giving scandal or causing injury to my neighbor. Slavish fear is not even referred to in the Exercises, yet deserves consideration at least for the historical reason that Luther and his followers falsely accused the Church of teaching that mere apprehension of divine punishment with no detachment of the will from sin is virtuous and salutary in the eyes of God.

Servile fear, unlike the slavish, not only shrinks from the pain that follows upon sin, but has the positive effect of detaching the will from affection for sinful creatures and keeping it attached to the will of God. Fear of this kind is praiseworthy and highly practical in resisting temptation, particularly where neglect or the strength of passion has weakened the motivating power of the love of God. Ignatius says it will help a man "escape from mortal sin," which isolates the main role of servile fear, apart from its use as a minimal basis for sacramental absolution. Psychologists say that under the stress of violent emotion, only a comparably strong emotion can neutralize the undesirable feeling-state and prevent its overriding right reason. Something of this kind takes place when servile fear is used to conquer temptation, whose pleasant character exerts a powerful attraction, via the feelings, on the human will. Unless measures are promptly taken to counteract the seduction, the will is liable to give in. Ideally the virtue of charity and a desire to please God alone should neutralize the attractiveness of a prospective sin. But my love of God may not be sufficiently deep to effect the counteraction or, if deep as a virtue, may be unable to act because passion keeps it from rising to the surface of consciousness. The fear of God, on the other hand, is so elemental and instinctive, that if a man has even a spark of faith he should be able to rouse his sense of anticipated pain and counterpoise the pleasure-feelings of the temptation.

However, servile fear has another purpose beyond its ability to resist temptation. It can easily develop into filial or reverential fear, "which is altogether acceptable and pleasing to God because it is inseparable from divine love." St. Thomas distinguishes these two fears according to the different evils that each of them seeks to avoid. In servile fear, the evil dreaded is punishment; in reverential the fear of offending God. But on closer analysis both types are seen to proceed from the love of God, although filial fear is *par excellence* inspired by pure charity, and, in that sense, "inseparable from divine love." When I dread the loss of heaven and the pains of hell, my fear, though servile, is basically motivated by the love of God whom I am afraid of losing by my sins, since heaven is the possession of God and hell the loss of Him for eternity. To that extent, therefore, even servile fear cannot be dissociated from supernatural charity. On a higher plane, however, when the object of my fear is not personal loss, though it be heaven, but injury to the Divine Majesty, then clearly the motive is not only an implicit love of God but love to a sublime degree.

The sources of divine charity from which servile and filial fear arise correspond to the familiar distinction between perfect and imperfect love of God, the one of benevolence and the other of concupiscence. In the pure love of benevolence, I love God for Himself alone, and not for any benefit He can bestow upon me. To this corresponds filial fear, wherein I dread to offend God, whom I love above all things, because I know that sin would "deprive" Him of the only good I can "give" Him, which is the gift of my voluntary affection. In the love of concupiscence, my love is egotistic. I love God because of the good things, including Himself, that attachment to His will can bring me. To this corresponds the servile fear that causes me to dread the loss of those very things to which the love of concupiscence inclines me.

Against this background we can understand how readily servile fear may become filial, much as imperfect love can develop into perfect charity. I begin by fearing the pain that God may send me if I commit a mortal sin. The crisis of temptation passes away and spontaneously I am grateful for being delivered from my folly and escaping the consequences of the sin. Since gratitude is the normal food of love, when the reason for being thankful is deliverance from the greatest possible evil, the result is—or should be—the greatest possible love.

Appendix I

Selections from the Text of the Exercises

FIRST PRINCIPLE AND FOUNDATION

Man is created to praise, reverence, and serve God our Lord, and by this means to save his soul.

The other things on the face of the earth are created for man to help him in attaining the end for which he is created.

Hence, man is to make use of them in as far as they help him in the attainment of his end, and he must rid himself of them in as far as they prove a hindrance to him.

Therefore, we must make ourselves indifferent to all created things, as far as we are allowed free choice and are not under any prohibition. Consequently, as far as we are concerned, we should not prefer health to sickness, riches to poverty, honor to dishonor, a long life to a short life. The same holds for all other things.

Our one desire and choice should be what is more conducive to the end for which we are created.

SIN: ANGELIC, ORIGINAL AND PERSONAL

The First Exercise is a meditation on the first, second, and third sin, employing the three powers of the soul. After the preparatory prayer and two preludes, it contains three principal points and a colloquy.

In the preparatory prayer I will beg of God our Lord that all my intentions, actions and operations may be directed purely to the praise and service of His Divine Majesty.

FIRST PRELUDE. This is a mental representation of the place.
. . . In a case where the subject matter is not visible, as here
in a meditation on sin, the representation will be to see in
imagination my soul as a prisoner in this corruptible body, and
to consider my whole composite being as an exile here on
earth, cast out to live among brute beasts. I said my whole
composite being, body and soul.

SECOND PRELUDE. I will ask God our Lord for what I want
and desire. . . . Here it will be to ask for shame and confusion, because I see how many have been lost on account of a
single mortal sin, and how many times I have deserved eternal
damnation, because of the many grievous sins that I have committed.

THE FIRST POINT. This will consist in using the memory to recall the first sin, which was that of the angels, and then in
applying the understanding by reasoning upon this sin, then
the will by seeking to remember and understand all to be the
more filled with shame and confusion when I compare the one
sin of the angels with the many sins I have committed. I will
consider that they went to hell for one sin, and the number of
times I have deserved to be condemned forever because of my
numerous sins.

I said we should apply the memory to the sin of the angels,
that is, recalling that they were created in the state of grace,
that they did not want to make use of the freedom God gave
them to reverence and obey their Creator and Lord, and so
falling into pride, were changed from grace to hatred of God,
and cast out of heaven into hell.

So, too, the understanding is to be used to think over the
matter more in detail, and then the will to rouse more deeply
the emotions.

SECOND POINT. In the same way the three powers of the soul
are to be applied to the sin of Adam and Eve. Recall to memory how on account of this sin they did penance for so long a
time, and the great corruption which came upon the human
race that caused so many to be lost in hell.

I said recall to mind the second sin, that of our First Parents. After Adam had been created on the Plain of Damascus and placed in the Garden of Paradise, and Eve had been formed from his side, they sinned by violating the command not to eat of the tree of knowledge. Thereafter, they were clothed in garments of skin and cast out of Paradise. By their sin they lost original justice, and for the rest of their lives, lived without it in many labors and great penance.

So, too, the understanding is to be used to think over the matter in greater detail, and the will is to be used as explained above.

THIRD POINT. In like manner we are to do the same with regard to the third sin, namely, that of one who went to hell because of one mortal sin. Consider also countless others who have been lost for fewer sins than I have committed.

I said to do the same for the third particular sin. Recall to memory the gravity and malice of sin against our Creator and Lord. Use the understanding in considering that because of sin, and of acting against the Infinite Goodness, one is justly condemned forever. Close with the acts of the will as we have said above.

COLLOQUY. Imagine Christ our Lord present before you upon the cross, and begin to speak with him, asking how it is that though He is the Creator, He has stooped to become man, and to pass from eternal life to death here in time, that thus He might die for our sins.

I shall also reflect upon myself and ask:

"What have I done for Christ?

"What am I doing for Christ?

"What ought I to do for Christ?"

As I behold Christ in this plight, nailed to the cross, I shall ponder upon what presents itself to my mind. . . .

The colloquy is made by speaking exactly as one friend speaks to another, or as a servant speaks to a master, now asking him for a favor, now blaming himself for some misdeed, now making known his affairs to him, and seeking advice in them. Close with an *Our Father.*

SECOND EXERCISE. This is a meditation on our sins. After the preparatory prayer and two preludes, there are five points and a colloquy.

FIRST PRELUDE. This will be the same as in the First Exercise.

SECOND PRELUDE. This is to ask for what I desire. Here it will be to ask for a growing and intense sorrow and tears for my sins.

FIRST POINT. This is a record of my sins. I will call to mind all the sins of my life, reviewing year by year, and period by period. Three things will help me in this: First, to consider the place where I lived; secondly, my dealings with others; thirdly, the office I have held.

SECOND POINT. I will weigh the gravity of my sins, and see the loathsomeness and malice which every mortal sin I have committed has in itself, even though it were not forbidden.

THIRD POINT. I will consider who I am, and by means of examples humble myself:

What am I compared with all men?

What are all men compared with the angels and saints of paradise?

Consider what all creation is in comparison with God. Then I alone, what can I be?

I will consider all the corruption and loathsomeness of my body.

I will consider myself as a source of corruption and contagion from which have issued countless sins and the most offensive poison.

FOURTH POINT. I will consider who God is against whom I have sinned, going through His attributes and comparing them with their contraries in me: His wisdom with my ignorance, His power with my weakness, His justice with my iniquity, His goodness with my wickedness.

FIFTH POINT. This is a cry of wonder accompanied by surging emotion as I pass in review all creatures. How is it that they have permitted me to live, and have sustained me in life! Why have the angels, though they are the sword of God's justice, tolerated me, guarded me, and prayed for me! Why have the saints interceded for me and asked favors for me! And the heavens, sun, moon, stars, and the elements; fruits, birds, fishes, and other animals—why have they all been at my service! How is it that the earth did not open to swallow me up, and create new hells in which I should be tormented forever!

COLLOQUY. I will conclude with a colloquy, extolling the mercy of God our Lord, pouring out my thoughts to Him, and giving thanks to Him that up to this very moment He has granted me life. I will resolve with His grace to amend for the future. Close with an *Our Father*.

The Third Exercise is a repetition of the First and Second Exercises with three colloquies.

After the preparatory prayer and the two preludes, this exercise will consist in repeating the First and Second Exercise. In doing this, we should pay attention to and dwell upon those points in which we have experienced greater consolation or desolation or greater spiritual appreciation. After the repetition, three colloquies are to be used in the following manner:

FIRST COLLOQUY. The first colloquy will be with our Blessed Lady, that she may obtain grace for me from her Son for three favors:

1. a deep knowledge of my sins and a feeling of abhorrence for them;

2. an understanding of the disorder of my actions, that filled with horror of them, I may amend my life and put it in order;

3. a knowledge of the world, that filled with horror, I may put away from me all that is worldly and vain. Then I will say a *Hail Mary*.

SECOND COLLOQUY. I will make the same petitions to the Divine Son that He may obtain these graces for me from the Father. After that I will say *Soul of Christ*.

THIRD COLLOQUY. I will make the same requests of the heav-

enly Father that He Himself may grant them to me. Then I
will close with the *Our Father*.

THE KINGDOM OF CHRIST

FIRST PRELUDE. This is a mental representation of the place.
Here it will be to see in imagination the synagogues, villages
and towns where Jesus preached.

SECOND PRELUDE. I will ask for the grace I desire. Here it will
be to ask of our Lord the grace not to be deaf to His call, but
prompt and diligent to accomplish His holy will.

Call of an Earthly King

FIRST POINT. This will be to place before my mind a human
king, chosen by God our Lord Himself, to whom all Christian
princes and people pay homage and obedience.

SECOND POINT. This will be to consider the address this king
makes to all his subjects, with the words: "It is my will to
conquer all infidel lands. Therefore, whoever wishes to join
with me in this enterprise must be content with the same food,
drink, clothing, etc. as mine. So, too, he must work with me
by day, and watch with me by night, etc., that as he has had a
share in the toil with me, afterwards, he may share in the victory with me."

THIRD POINT. Consider what the answer of good subjects
ought to be to a king so generous and nobleminded, and consequently, if anyone would refuse the invitation of such a king,
how justly he would deserve to be condemned by the whole
world, and looked upon as an ignoble knight.

Call of Christ the Eternal King. The second part of this exercise will consist in applying the example of the earthly king
mentioned above to Christ our Lord according to the following points:

FIRST POINT. If such a summons of an earthly king to his subjects deserves our attention, how much more worthy of consideration is Christ our Lord, the Eternal King, before whom is
assembled the whole world. To all His summons goes forth,

and to each one in particular He addresses the words: "It is my will to conquer the whole world and all my enemies, and thus to enter into the glory of my Father. Therefore, whoever wishes to join me in this enterprise must be willing to labor with me, that by following me in suffering, he may follow me in glory."

SECOND POINT. Consider that all persons who have judgment and reason will offer themselves entirely for this work.

THIRD POINT. Those who wish to give greater proof of their love, and to distinguish themselves in the service of the eternal King and the Lord of all, will not only offer themselves entirely for the work, but will act against their sensuality and carnal and worldly love, and make offerings of greater value and of more importance in words such as these:

Eternal Lord of all things, in the presence of Thy infinite goodness, and of Thy glorious mother, and of all the saints of Thy heavenly court, this is the offering of myself which I make with Thy favor and help. I protest that it is my earnest desire and my deliberate choice, provided only it is for Thy greater service and praise, to imitate Thee in bearing all wrongs and all abuse and all poverty, both actual and spiritual, should Thy most holy majesty deign to choose and admit me to such a state and way of life.

TWO STANDARDS

The one of Christ, our supreme leader and lord, the other of Lucifer, the deadly enemy of our human nature.

FIRST PRELUDE. This is the history. Here it will be that Christ calls and wants all beneath His standard, and Lucifer, on the other hand, wants all under his.

SECOND PRELUDE. This is a mental representation. It will be here to see a great plain, comprising the whole region about Jerusalem, where the sovereign Commander-in-Chief of all the good is Christ our Lord; and another plain about the region of Babylon, where the chief of the enemy is Lucifer.

THIRD PRELUDE. This is to ask for what I desire. Here it will be to ask for a knowledge of the deceits of the rebel chief and help to guard myself against them; and also to ask for a knowl-

edge of the true life exemplified in the sovereign and true
Commander, and the grace to imitate Him.

Standard of Satan

FIRST POINT. Imagine you see the chief of all the enemy in
the vast plain about Babylon, seated on a great throne of fire
and smoke, his appearance inspiring horror and terror.

SECOND POINT. Consider how he summons innumerable demons, and scatters them, some to one city and some to another, throughout the whole world, so that no province, no
place, no state of life, no individual is overlooked.

THIRD POINT. Consider the address he makes to them, how
he goads them on to lay snares for men, to seek to chain them.
First they are to tempt them to covet riches (as Satan himself
is accustomed to do in most cases) that they may the more
easily attain the empty honors of this world, and then come to
over-weening pride.

The first step, then, will be riches, the second honor, the
third pride. From these three steps the evil one leads to all
other vices.

Standard of Christ

In a similar way we are to picture to ourselves the sovereign
and true Commander, Christ our Lord.

FIRST POINT. Consider Christ our Lord, standing in a lowly
place in a great plain about the region of Jerusalem, His appearance beautiful and attractive.

SECOND POINT. Consider how the Lord of all the world
chooses so many persons, apostles, disciples, etc., and sends
them throughout the whole world to spread His sacred doctrine among all men, no matter what their state or condition.

THIRD POINT. Consider the address which Christ our Lord
makes to His servants and friends whom He sends on this enterprise, recommending to them to seek to help all, first by
attracting them to the highest spiritual poverty, and should it
please the Divine Majesty, and should He deign to choose
them for it, even to actual poverty. Secondly, they should lead

them to a desire for insults and contempt, for from these
springs humility.

COLLOQUY. A colloquy should be addressed to our Lady, asking her to obtain for me from her Son and Lord to be received
under His standard, first in the highest spiritual poverty, and
should the Divine Majesty be pleased thereby, even in actual
poverty; secondly, in bearing insults and wrongs, thereby to
imitate Him better, provided only I can suffer these without
sin on the part of another, and without offense of the Divine
Majesty. Then I will say the *Hail Mary.*

SECOND COLLOQUY. This will be to ask her Son to obtain the
same favors for me from the Father. Then I will say, *Soul of
Christ.*

THIRD COLLOQUY. This will be to beg the Father to grant
me the same graces. Then I will say the *Our Father.*

THREE CLASSES OF MEN

FIRST PRELUDE. This is a history of the Three Classes of
Men. Each of them has acquired ten thousand ducats, but not
entirely as they should have, for the love of God. They all wish
to save their souls and find peace in God our Lord by ridding
themselves of the burden arising from the attachment to the
sum acquired, which impedes the attainment of this end.

SECOND PRELUDE. This is a mental representation of the
place. Here it will be to behold myself standing in the presence
of God our Lord and of all His saints to desire and know what
is more pleasing to His Divine Goodness.

THIRD PRELUDE. This is to ask for what I desire. Here it will
be to beg for the grace to choose what is more for the glory of
His Divine Majesty and the salvation of my soul.

THE FIRST CLASS. They would like to rid themselves of the
attachment they have to the sum acquired in order to find
peace in God our Lord and assure their salvation, but the hour
of death comes, and they have not made use of any means.

THE SECOND CLASS. They want to rid themselves of the attachment, but they wish to do so in such a way that they retain

what they have acquired, so that God is to come to what they desire, and they do not decide to give up the sum of money in order to go to God, though this would be the better way for them.

THE THIRD CLASS. These want to rid themselves of the attachment, but they wish to do so in such a way that they desire neither to retain nor to relinquish the sum acquired. They seek only to will and not will as God our Lord inspires them, and as seems better for the service and praise of the Divine Majesty. Meanwhile, they will strive to conduct themselves as if every attachment to it had been broken. They will make efforts neither to want that, nor anything else, unless the service of God our Lord alone move them to do so. As a result, the desire to be better able to serve God our Lord will be the cause of their accepting anything or relinquishing it.

THREEFOLD COLLOQUY. I will make use of the same three colloquies employed in the preceding contemplation on the Two Standards.

It should be noted that when we feel an attachment opposed to actual poverty or a repugnance to it, when we are not indifferent to poverty and riches, it will be very helpful in order to overcome the inordinate attachment, even though corrupt nature rebel against it, to beg our Lord in the colloquies to choose us to serve Him in actual poverty. We should insist that we desire it, beg for it, plead for it, provided, of course, that it be for the service and praise of the Divine Goodness.

THREE KINDS OF HUMILITY

THE FIRST KIND OF HUMILITY. This is necessary for salvation. It consists in this, that as far as possible I so subject and humble myself as to obey the law of God our Lord in all things, so that not even were I made lord of all creation, or to save my life here on earth, would I consent to violate a commandment, whether divine or human, that binds me under pain of mortal sin.

THE SECOND KIND OF HUMILITY. This is more perfect than the

first. I possess it if my attitude of mind is such that I neither desire nor am I inclined to have riches rather than poverty, to seek honor rather than dishonor, to desire a long life rather than a short life, provided only in either alternative I would promote equally the service of God our Lord and the salvation of my soul. Besides this indifference, this second kind of humility supposes that not for all creation, nor to save my life, would I consent to commit a venial sin.

THE THIRD KIND OF HUMILITY. This is the most perfect. It consists in this. If we suppose the first and second kind attained, then whenever the praise and glory of God would be equally served, I desire and choose poverty with Christ poor, rather than riches, in order to imitate and be in reality more like Christ our Lord; I choose insults with Christ loaded with them, rather than honors; I desire to be accounted as worthless and a fool for Christ, rather than to be esteemed as wise and prudent in this world. So Christ was treated before me.

NOTE. If one desires to attain this third kind of humility, it will help very much to use the three colloquies at the close of the meditation on the three Classes of Men mentioned above. He should beg our Lord to deign to choose him for this third kind of humility, which is higher and better, that he may the more imitate and serve Him, provided equal praise and service be given to the Divine Majesty.

TWO WAYS OF MAKING AN ELECTION

The First Way

FIRST POINT I place before my mind the object with regard to which I wish to make a choice, for example, an office, or the reception or rejection of a benefice, or anything else that may be the object of a choice subject to change.

SECOND POINT. It is necessary to keep as my aim the end for which I am created, that is, the praise of God and the salvation of my soul. Besides this, I must be indifferent, without any inordinate attachment, so that I am not more inclined or disposed to accept the object in question than to relinquish it, nor to give it up than to accept it. I should be like a balance at equilibrium, without leaning to either side, that I might be ready to follow whatever I perceive is more for the glory and praise of God and the salvation of my soul.

THIRD POINT. I should beg God our Lord to deign to move my will, and to bring to my mind what I ought to do to promote His praise and glory with regard to the matter in question. Then I should use the understanding to weigh the matter with care and fidelity, and make my choice in conformity with His most holy will.

FOURTH POINT. This will be to weigh the matter by reckoning the number of advantages and benefits that would accrue to me if I had the proposed office or benefice solely for the praise of God our Lord and the salvation of my soul. On the other hand, I should weigh the disadvantages and dangers there might be in having it. I will do the same with the second alternative, that is, weigh the advantages and benefits as well as the disadvantages and danger of not having it.

FIFTH POINT. After I have gone over and pondered in this way every aspect of the matter in question, I will consider which alternative appears more reasonable. Then I must come to a decision in the matter under deliberation because of weightier motives presented to my reason, and not because of any sensual inclination.

SIXTH POINT. After such a choice or decision, the one who has made it must turn with great diligence to prayer in the presence of God our Lord, and offer Him his choice that the Divine Majesty may deign to accept and confirm it if it is for His greater service and praise.

The Second Way

FIRST RULE. The love that moves and causes one to choose must descend from above, that is, from the love of God, so that before one chooses he should perceive that the greater or less attachment for the object of his choice is solely because of His Creator and Lord.

SECOND RULE. I should represent to myself a man whom I have never seen or known, and whom I would like to see practice all perfection. Then I should consider what I would tell him to do and choose for the greater glory of God our Lord and the greater perfection of his soul. I will do the same, and keep the rule I propose to others.

THIRD RULE. This is to consider what procedure and norm of action I would wish to have followed in making the present choice if I were at the moment of death. I will guide myself by this and make my decision entirely in conformity with it.

FOURTH RULE. Let me picture and consider myself as standing in the presence of my judge on the last day, and reflect what decision in the present matter I would then wish to have made. I will choose now the rule of life that I would then wish to have observed, that on the day of judgment I may be filled with happiness and joy.

Guided by the rules given above for my eternal salvation and peace, I will make my decision, and will offer it to God our Lord.

DIRECTIONS FOR AMENDMENT AND REFORMATION IN ONE'S STATE OF LIFE

It must be borne in mind that some may be established in an ecclesiastical office, or may be married, and hence cannot make a choice of a state of life, or, in matters that may be changed and hence are subject to a choice, they may not be ready to make one.

It will be profitable for such persons, whether they possess great wealth or not, in place of a choice, to propose a way for each to reform his manner of living in his state by setting before him the purpose of his creation and of his life and position, namely, the glory of God our Lord and the salvation of his soul.

If he is really to attain this end, during the Exercises and during the consideration of the ways of making an election as explained above, he will have to examine and weigh in all its details how large a household he should maintain, how he ought to direct and administer it, how he ought to teach its members by word and example. So too he should consider what part of his income should be used for his family and household, and how much should be set aside for distribution to the poor and other pious practices.

Let him desire and seek nothing except the greater praise and glory of God our Lord as the aim of all he does. For every one must keep in mind that he will make progress in all that concerns the spiritual life in proportion as he shall have divested himself of self-love, and of his own will and interests.

CONTEMPLATION TO ATTAIN THE LOVE OF GOD

NOTE. Before starting this exercise, it will be good to call attention to two points:

1. The first is that love should be manifested in deeds rather than words.

2. The second is that love consists in a mutual sharing of goods, for example, the lover gives and shares with the beloved what he possesses, or something of that which he has or is able to give; and vice versa, the beloved shares with the lover. Hence, if one has knowledge, he shares it with the one who does not possess it; and so also if one has honors, or riches. Thus, one always gives to the other.

FIRST PRELUDE. This is a representation of the place, which here is to behold myself standing in the presence of God our Lord and of His angels and saints, who intercede for me.

SECOND PRELUDE. This is to ask for what I desire. Here it will be to ask for an intimate knowledge of the many blessings received, that filled with gratitude for all, I may in all things love and serve the Divine Majesty.

FIRST POINT. This is to recall to mind the blessings of creation and redemption, and the special favors I have received.

I will ponder with great affection how much God our Lord has done for me, and how much He has given me of what He possesses, and finally, how much, as far as He can, the same Lord desires to give Himself to me according to His divine decrees.

Then I will reflect upon myself, and consider, according to all reason and justice, what I ought to offer the Divine Majesty, that is, all I possess and myself with it. Thus, as one would do who is moved by great feeling, I will make this offering of myself:

Take, O Lord, and receive all my liberty, my memory, my understanding, and all my will, whatsoever I have and possess. Thou hast given all these things to me; to Thee, O Lord, I restore them: all are Thine, dispose of them all according to Thy will. Give me Thy love and Thy grace, for this is enough for me.

SECOND POINT. This is to reflect how God dwells in creatures: in the elements giving them existence, in the plants giving them life, in the animals conferring upon them sensation, in man bestowing understanding. So He dwells in me and gives me being, life, sensation, intelligence, and makes a temple of me, besides having created me in the likeness and image of the Divine Majesty.

Then I will reflect upon myself again in the manner stated in the first point, or in some other way that may seem better.

The same should be observed with regard to each of the points that follow.

THIRD POINT. This is to consider how God works and labors for me in all creatures upon the face of the earth, that is, He conducts Himself as one who labors. Thus, in the elements, plants, fruits and cattle, He gives being, conserves them, confers life and sensation.

Then I will reflect on myself.

FOURTH POINT. This is to consider all blessings and gifts as descending from above. Thus, my limited power comes from the supreme and infinite power above, and so, too, my justice, goodness, mercy, etc., descend from above as the rays of light descend from the sun, and as the waters flow from their fountains.

Then I will reflect on myself as has been said.

Conclude with a colloquy and the *Our Father.**

* With minor changes, the foregoing selections are from the English translation of the Spiritual Exercises by Rev. Louis J. Puhl, S.J., published by the Newman Press.

Appendix II

*Apostolic Constitution of Pius XI
Declaring St. Ignatius Patron of
All Spiritual Exercises*

It has always been the chief concern of the Sovereign Pontiffs to commend, and highly to praise, to promote, and strongly to encourage, all that notably makes for the goodness and perfection of Christian life. Now a place in the front rank of all that helps towards this end has been won by those Spiritual Exercises which St. Ignatius, by a certain divine instinct, introduced into the Church. For although, in the goodness and mercy of God, men have never been wanting to set forth aptly deep thoughts upon heavenly things before the eyes of the faithful, yet Ignatius was the first to begin to teach a certain system and special method of going through spiritual retreats. He did this in the little book which he wrote when he was still a quite uneducated man, and to which he himself gave the name "Spiritual Exercises." This method was such as wonderfully to help the faithful to hate sin, and to plan out their life holily after the model of our Lord Jesus Christ.

To the power of the Ignatian method is due the fact that, as Our eminent Predecessor Leo XIII avowed, the high value of these Exercises has been proved by the experience of the last three centuries and by the witness of all who during that time gave evidence of the highest form of ascetical training and holiness of life. Along with the many shining examples

197

of holiness actually found in the household of St. Ignatius itself, who expressly declare that it is from the Exercises, as its
source, that they have drawn their whole plan of asceticism,
we love also to recall, from among the secular clergy, those
two lights of the Church, St. Francis of Sales and St. Charles
Borromeo. Francis, when seeking duly to prepare himself for
episcopal consecration, carefully retired in order to make the
Ignatian Exercises, and during them mapped out for himself
that plan of life, to which he afterwards remained always faithful, according to the principles for the "Reformation of Life"
contained in St. Ignatius' little book. Charles Borromeo, as
Our Predecessor of happy memory, Pius X, has shown, and as
We Ourselves have proved in historical papers published before We were raised to the Supreme Pontificate, having experienced the value of the Exercises in his own person and
being led by them to adopt a more perfect form of life, went
on to spread their use abroad among clergy and laity alike.
Among holy men and women belonging to religious bodies,
it will be enough to quote, for example, that mistress of lofty
contemplation, Teresa, and Leonard of Port Maurice, the son
of the Seraphic Patriarch, who rated St. Ignatius' book so
highly that he owned he wholly followed its plan when win-
ning souls to God.

Accordingly this book—so small in bulk, yet so marvelous—
from its first edition has been solemnly approved by the Roman Pontiffs. They have praised it most highly, have sanc-
tioned it by their Apostolic Authority, and have constantly
urged men to use it by means of numerous indulgences and
the recommendation of frequent encomiums.

We regard it as certain that most of the ills of our day start
from the fact that "no one reflects in his heart." We deem it
proved that the Spiritual Exercises, made according to the plan
of St. Ignatius, have the greatest efficacy in dispelling the most
stubborn difficulties with which human society is now confronted. We have studied the rich harvest of virtues that ripens
today no less than of old in spiritual retreats, not only among

members of religious congregations and the secular clergy, but also among the laity, and, what in our day is worthy of special and separate remark, among the working classes themselves. Therefore We earnestly wish that the making of these Spiritual Exercises should daily spread more widely. We also desire that retreat houses, where persons withdraw for a whole month, or for eight days, or for fewer, there to put themselves into training for the perfect Christian life, may come into being and flourish everywhere more numerously.

This in Our love for the Lord's flock We beg from God. And therefore, in answer to the earnest desires and petitions of the Sacred Hierarchy of both rites in practically the whole Catholic world, and also because We Ourselves are eager to give no doubtful sign of Our gratitude towards the Holy Patriarch at this time, particularly on the occasion of the third centenary of the canonization of St. Ignatius and the fourth centenary of the writing of this invaluable little book, following the example of Our Predecessors who have assigned patrons and guardians to various institutions, having called a council of Our Venerable Brethren, the Cardinals of the Holy Roman Catholic Church who preside over the Congregation of Sacred Rites, We, by Our Apostolic Authority, declare, constitute and proclaim St. Ignatius of Loyola to be the Heavenly Patron of all Spiritual Exercises, and accordingly of all institutes, Sodalities, or groups of whatever sort, which bestow their care and zeal upon those who are making the Spiritual Exercises.

And We decree that these Our Letters are and ever will be firm, valid and efficacious, and that to them belong and shall accrue their proper, full and integral effects, notwithstanding anything whatsoever to the contrary.

Given at Rome, at St. Peter's, in the year of Our Lord 1922, the 25th day of July, the first of Our Pontificate.

Pius P.P. XI

Index

A NOTE ON THE TYPE

IN WHICH THIS BOOK WAS SET

This book has been set in Electra, a type face created in 1935 by W. A. Dwiggins, the well-known Boston artist. This type falls within the "modern" family of type styles, but was drawn to avoid the extreme contrast between "thick and thin" elements that marks most "modern" type faces. The design is not based upon any traditional model, and is not an attempt to revive or to reconstruct any historic type. Since its birth, Electra has met with success because of its easy-to-read quality. This book was composed and printed by the York Composition Company, Inc., of York, and bound by Moore and Company of Baltimore. The design and typography of this book are by Howard N. King.